AROUND THE TABLE

TABLES & TRADITIONS FOR GATHERING

by SHEA McGEE *with* KATIE CALTON

photography by LUCY CALL

AROUND THE TABLE

TABLES & TRADITIONS FOR GATHERING

HARPER HORIZON

For my family,

You have made our kitchen a place of joy and our table a sanctuary of connection.

Thank you for graciously moving through every creative pursuit and culinary adventure alongside me.

This book is for you—my trusted critics, my constant inspiration, my heart.

Around the Table:
Tables & Traditions for Gathering

Published by Harper Horizon, an imprint of HarperCollins Focus LLC, 501 Nelson Place, Nashville, TN 37214, USA.

ISBN (HC): 978-1-4002-5062-2
ISBN (ePub): 978-1-4002-5063-9
ISBN (CE): 978-1-4041-2205-5

HarperCollins Publishers, Macken House, 39/40 Mayor Street Upper, Dublin 1, D01 C9W8, Ireland (https://www.harpercollins.com)

Library of Congress Control Number: 2025947516

Art direction: Belinda Bass
Cover design and interior design: Kortney Eggertz
Photography: Lucy Call

Printed in Italy

26 27 28 29 30 RTL 5 4 3 2 1

CONTENTS

	Introduction	13
	Styling	19
SPRING	Garden Brunch	34
	Farmers Market Lunch	50
	Celebration Dinner	66
	Spring Fête	76
SUMMER	Alfresco Evening	96
	Backyard Barbeque	112
	Classic Seafood Boil	128
	Pizza Night	140
	Beach Picnic	162
FALL	Harvest Dinner	178
	Annual Pie Night	196
	Soup Bar	218
	Autumn Evening at Home	236
WINTER	Christmas Morning	252
	Cookie Exchange	262
	Holiday Dinner Party	282
	Date Night	296
	Weeknight Meals	308
	Acknowledgments	326
	Recipe Index	328

SPRING

GARDEN BRUNCH
Vegetable Frittata 37
White Bean Hummus with Walnut Oil 39
Loaded Everyday Granola 41
Whipped Ricotta Crostini 43
No-Bake Bay Leaf Cheesecake 45
Rosy Mimosas 47

FARMERS MARKET LUNCH
Whole Wheat Focaccia 53
Market BLTA 57
Strawberry Tabbouleh 59
Tzatziki Cucumbers 61
Shea's Favorite Chocolate Chip Cookie 63

CELEBRATION DINNER
Tender Grilled Flank Steak 69
Farro Arugula Salad 71
Confetti Birthday Blondies 73

SPRING FÊTE
Melt-in-Your-Mouth Salmon with Asparagus 79
Lemony Smashed Potatoes 81
Butter Lettuce Salad 83
Basil Garlic Knots 85
Four-Layer Southern Coconut Cake 87

SUMMER

ALFRESCO EVENING
Cast-Iron Piccata 99
Garden Couscous Salad 101
Apple & Brie Bites 103
Baguette with Balsamic Dipping Oil 105
Lemon Berry Pavlova 107

BACKYARD BARBEQUE
Syd's Sliders for a Crowd 115
Grilled Squash with Whipped Feta 119
Charred Corn Salad with Cilantro Dressing 121
Grandma Glo's Cola Cake 123
Watermelon Ranch Water 125

CLASSIC SEAFOOD BOIL
Classic Seafood Boil 131
Grilled Garlic Bread 133
Strawberries & Cream Cake 135
Arnold Palmer 137

PIZZA NIGHT
Perfect Pizza Dough 143
Go-To Tomato Sauce 145
Fontina Apple Pizza 147
Hot Honey Pizza 149
Green Goddess Pizza 151
Sausage & Mushroom Pizza 153
Peach Burrata Salad 155
S'mores Cookie Skillet 157
Salted Vanilla Bean Ice Cream 159

BEACH PICNIC
Turkey Beach Sandwich with Kale Cashew Pesto 165
Blackberry Gouda Skewers 167
Picnic Potato Chips 169
McGee's Ultimate Brownie 171

FALL

HARVEST DINNER

Essential Roasted Turkey 181
Autumn Sweet Potato Salad 185
Golden Crescent Rolls 187
Brown Butter Green Beans with Crunchy Breadcrumbs 191
Gruyère Brioche Stuffing 193

ANNUAL PIE NIGHT

Guide to Charcuterie 199
Reliably Flaky Pie Crust 201
Chocolate Hazelnut Meringue Pie 203
Pumpkin-Pie Cheesecake Bars 207
Mixed Berry Slab Pie 209
Brown Butter Pecan Pie 213

SOUP BAR

Chicken Tortilla Soup 221
Roasted Red Pepper & Tortellini Soup 223
Cauliflower Corn Chowder 225
Beef Pot Pie Soup 227
Turkey & Wild Rice Soup 231
Cornbread Bundts with Rosemary Honey Butter 233

AUTUMN EVENING AT HOME

Butternut Squash Enchiladas 239
Crunchy Cabbage Slaw 243
Magic Crispy Bars 245

WINTER

CHRISTMAS MORNING

Savory Dutch Baby 255
Mini Cinnamon Rolls 257
Citrus & Fennel Salad 259

COOKIE EXCHANGE

Chocolate Peppermint Sandwich Cookies 265
Snowball Sandies 269
White Chocolate Chewy Gingersnaps 271
Cookie Butter Blossoms 275
Cream Cheese Spritz Wreaths 277
Triple-Chocolate Hot Chocolate 279

HOLIDAY DINNER PARTY

Cranberry Braised Short Ribs 285
Cacio e Pepe Mashed Potatoes 287
Winter Salad with Tahini Dressing 289
Brown Butter Citrus Cake 291

DATE NIGHT

Silky Mascarpone Pappardelle 299
Caesar Salad with Crispy Chickpeas 301
Cherry Chocolate Mousse 303
Pomegranate Sangria 305

WEEKNIGHT MEALS

Garlicky Cod & Quinoa 311
Broccoli Pistachio Spaghetti 313
Tajín Ranch Chicken Thighs 315
Sheet Pan Lasagna Bolognese 317
Swiss "Charred" Portobello Bowls 319
Plum & Fennel Pork Chops 321
Greek Halloumi & Chicken Salad 323
Roasted Chicken with Lemon Orzotto 325

INTRODUCTION

I am an interior designer, not a professionally trained chef. For more than a decade, I have designed homes and products known for their balance of luxury and comfort. Like any true creative, my design sensibilities are ever evolving, but I have always remained true to my love of classics with a twist. Think of a kitchen with Calacatta marble countertops, an apron-front sink, and a large crock overflowing with wooden spoons near the range. My style is elevated, yet laid-back; simple, but with an eye for detail.

Beyond the paint colors and furniture, what I really design are experiences that bring people together in their homes. And for me, a good experience usually (always) involves food. Long before I was immersed in the art of tablescapes adorned with French dinnerware and embroidered linen napkins, there was the table. Simple and pure—a place for gathering, long conversations, and a shared love of food and each other.

In my childhood home in Houston, Texas, weeknights were often spent carpooling to activities, with quick meals of cereal or sandwiches squeezed in between. But Sundays were different. Sundays were for slowing down and sitting together around the table. Sundays were also dessert days. My mom would let me climb onto the counter to help, flipping through a well-loved binder of torn-out recipes from *Southern Living* magazine for inspiration. Even now, Sunday dinner, Sunday desserts, and gathering friends and family around the table feels like a continuation of that tradition.

In 1999, my dad finally decided to spring for cable television. While my brother and I were thrilled to finally be up-to-date in pop culture, no one was more excited than my mom. The Food Network became her obsession. I remember the familiar voices of the chefs floating through the house, but it was *Barefoot Contessa* that we would actually sit down and watch together. I can still hum the intro song, and the nostalgia of Ina Garten making her husband, Jeffrey, his favorite roast chicken, then spending the evening in her backyard, never left me.

In the summers, we would visit my grandparents' farm in North Carolina and wake every morning to the smell of biscuits. My grandmother would rise before the sun, her kitchen bathed in the soft glow of light reflecting off the pond, a hummingbird buzzing by the feeder outside the window. I can still picture her at the narrow stretch of counter between the sink and the stove, moving with a quiet, practiced rhythm. There was a small crease at the base of her palm where she measured and rolled biscuit dough by feel. She had few written recipes and moved through the kitchen mostly by instinct—and copious amounts of butter and lard.

Grandma Glo introduced me to what it means to show your love through food. When our family visited, she would squeeze eight people around a table built for four. There were no elaborate tablescapes or floral arrangements, only the magic of a meal made with care, and the long nights spent laughing around a cramped table.

That spirit is what inspired this cookbook. It's a celebration of the seasons, the table, and the joy of gathering—whether it's around a table set with heirloom china, or one simply piled with good food and good company.

Years later, as a newlywed, I found myself at the start of a new kind of learning curve. My husband, Syd, was a self-proclaimed plain eater, preferring cheeseburgers with nothing on them, not even a piece of lettuce. I, on the other hand, knew how to make exactly two things: salads and cookies.

One meal at a time, year after year, I taught myself to cook by blending my love for fresh ingredients, comfort, and creating inviting atmospheres. I was determined to expand Syd's horizons, to build a home where the food was just as nurturing as the surroundings. Living in Orange County, California, I immersed myself in the abundance of organic produce, farmers markets, and vibrant flavors. I hooked him with homemade desserts and a steady understanding of comfort food. Little by little, our table grew fuller together.

What I didn't realize at the time was that the same creative instincts I trusted in my design work were guiding me in the kitchen. Following my passion for interiors, honing my aesthetic, layering textures, and blending beauty with comfort mirrored the way I was learning to cook—by feel, by intention, and with a deep appreciation for the full experience.

As my career in design grew, so did my experiences with food. Traveling across the country and abroad for projects and inspiration gave me countless opportunities to taste, to see, to learn—sometimes separately, but often all at once. I was constantly observing the way a thoughtfully designed environment could elevate a meal, and how a beautiful table could enhance even the simplest dish.

I often say that I want to design spaces that draw you in and beckon you to stay awhile, but what brings us together even more than a beautiful room? Food. Even better is food shared in a thoughtful environment, where every detail—the lighting, the linens, the menu—speaks the same quiet, welcoming language.

That's why my approach to cooking is as much about visuals and textures as it is about flavor. Just as I love airy interiors with layers of natural materials, I find myself drawn to cooking with fresh herbs, handpicked produce, and simple ingredients treated with care. I believe beauty belongs in every part of our lives—in the homes we design, the meals we serve, and the moments we create around the table.

In many ways, my love for design and my love for food have always been intertwined. Both are acts of creation; both rely on layering details with intention; and both invite others into an experience.

When I design a room, I think about how people will move through it, where they'll sit, what they'll reach for, and how they'll feel. Setting a table or preparing a meal is no different. It's about creating an atmosphere where people feel cared for—not only through beautiful surroundings but through the thoughtfulness woven into every element.

As I wrote this book, a question kept echoing in my mind: *Could I apply my design perspective to food?*

It didn't take long to realize that I already had.

The meals I love to cook—fresh, layered, seasonal—feel like an extension of the spaces I create. Thoughtful but unfussy, detailed yet comfortable, inviting by nature. In the same way a room tells a story through texture, light, and composition, a meal tells one through color, scent, and taste.

When I set a table with linen napkins worn soft with time, arrange a simple platter of ripe figs and honeycomb, or bring salmon to the table under a scattering of citrus and herbs, it feels like designing a moment that is meant to be lingered over, remembered, shared.

The food on these pages is more than a menu. It's another room I've created—open, welcoming, and filled with beauty you can taste and feel.

Design shapes how we live. Food shapes how we connect. Both, at their best, turn everyday moments into something memorable. I have always believed that a home should be both beautiful and lived in. Food, like design, sets the stage for those moments of real life to unfold.

The menus and tablescapes I've put together were thoughtfully paired. The ingredients flow together, and the scenes feel connected, but they're meant to be flexible. If you have time to make only one recipe, that's perfect. Pick and choose, mix and match, tailor it for your lifestyle.

Take note of the details—a table set with tiny potted plants, a charcuterie board layered with texture and color, cookies sprinkled with flaky salt—and make it your own.

I hope this book serves as inspiration for you to create your own traditions and design your own moments. Real beauty comes from gathering the people you love in spaces that feel like home. However you get there is exactly right.

Welcome to my table. I'm so glad you're here.

STYLING

Between us, I've hosted many dinners as an excuse to create a tablescape. I learn something new every time I open my home, and even when things don't go exactly as planned, I'm grateful for the opportunity to create a space where people can connect. It is my hosting philosophy that thoughtfulness, not perfection, should always be the goal.

Much like curating a thoughtfully layered room for a client, setting your table involves harmonizing function with aesthetic appeal—considering your guests, making choices that reflect the nature of the gathering, and styling in a way that complements rather than competes with the food. From florals that add softness and life, to linens that introduce texture and tone, every element plays a role in shaping the overall experience.

Whether you're preparing a casual weeknight dinner or an elegant holiday feast, intentional design choices transform your table into an inviting stage. My hope is that with a few simple styling tips, you'll be equipped to turn ordinary occasions into unforgettable gatherings.

Margot
Shea
Wren

STYLING: PANTRY

Build a collection of versatile table linens over time so you can effortlessly mix, match, and set the table without starting from scratch each time you host.

Pick up vintage serving pieces and tableware that speak to you to add character and a sense of story to your gatherings.

STYLING: TABLETOP

Vary the heights of serving pieces using cake stands, boards, and stacked dishes to create visual interest.

Mix textures and materials, like woven, polished, and matte finishes, to create a layered tablescape that feels collected and inviting.

STYLING: FLORAL

Combine juxtaposing textures—like delicate peonies with foraged greenery—for visual interest.

Style bud vases or small potted plants down the length of the table for a charming alternative to a single large arrangement.

LEFT: *Keep arrangements slightly asymmetrical to mimic nature and feel less formal.*

TIPS FOR HOSTING

TIP N^{O}. 1 Read the entire recipe from start to finish before you begin.

TIP N^{O}. 2 Anything that can be chopped, prepped, or placed ahead of time should be.

TIP N^{O}. 3 If possible, practice your tablescape and recipes beforehand to put your mind at ease.

TIP N^{O}. 4 Collect items over time, so you can effortlessly pull together a tablescape without starting from scratch.

TIP N^{O}. 5 Get to know your oven. Some run hot or cool or cook unevenly and you can make adjustments accordingly.

TIP N^{O}. 6 Always fluff, scoop, and level your flour to preserve the light, delicate texture every good bake depends on.

TIP N^{O}. 7 Using a digital meat thermometer will transform both your confidence and your food.

TIP N^{O}. 8 A little bit of greenery goes a long way to making a tablescape feel special—even if that means foraging for a few clippings from your yard.

TIP N^{O}. 9 When in doubt, garnish with leftover fresh herbs from the ingredient list.

TIP N^{O}. 10 Involving guests when they arrive relaxes the atmosphere and encourages conversation.

SPRING

GARDEN BRUNCH | FARMERS MARKET LUNCH
CELEBRATION DINNER | SPRING FÊTE

GARDEN BRUNCH

ON THE MENU

VEGETABLE FRITTATA

WHITE BEAN HUMMUS WITH WALNUT OIL

LOADED EVERYDAY GRANOLA

WHIPPED RICOTTA CROSTINI

NO-BAKE BAY LEAF CHEESECAKE

ROSY MIMOSAS

There's a quiet magic in the garden, a sense of calm and possibility as the earth stirs to life. Inspiration from nature has long guided my approach to design, and now, how I think about gathering and cooking.

These dishes are for brunch that stretches into lunch, tables scattered with rustic bread, chilled drinks catching the light, and simple, beautiful dishes meant to be shared. This setting feels as appropriate for a casual weekend gathering as it does for a bridal shower, baby shower, or any occasion worth savoring.

The menu captures that romantic spirit: a tender vegetable frittata; white bean hummus drizzled with warm, homemade walnut oil; granola tossed with bits of white chocolate; and airy whipped ricotta piped onto croissant crostini. For a luscious finish, a no-bake bay leaf cheesecake offers an herbaceous, unexpected twist, while rosy mimosas, kissed with a hint of rose water, invite you to toast in the morning.

STYLING: *Incorporate a few pieces with imperfections, like rustic wood boards and rumpled linens, to add an air of romance to a chic event.*

LODGE

YIELD: 8 SERVINGS   PREP: 25 MIN   COOK: 30 MIN

VEGETABLE FRITTATA

Fluffy eggs, garlic-sautéed veggies, and tangy goat cheese come together in a nutrient-packed frittata layered with the earthy flavors of broccoli, turnip, and leafy greens. Finished with a fresh scattering of microgreens, it's a vibrant option for brunch or a light dinner.

INGREDIENTS

1 pound fresh broccoli florets
½ medium turnip (about 1 cup finely diced)
¼ cup fresh basil leaves, loosely packed
4 garlic cloves
10 eggs
2 tablespoons water
¼ cup heavy whipping cream
1½ teaspoons kosher salt, divided
2 tablespoons extra-virgin olive oil
4 cups (4 ounces) chopped dandelion greens, Swiss chard, and/or kale
4 ounces goat cheese
3 ounces microgreens or pea shoots, for serving

DIRECTIONS

1. Preheat the oven to 375 degrees. Thinly slice the broccoli florets lengthwise and set aside. Dice the turnip, roughly chop the basil, and mince the garlic.

2. In a medium bowl whisk together the eggs, water, cream, and 1 teaspoon of the salt until no streaks remain.

3. Warm the olive oil in a 10-inch cast-iron skillet set over medium heat. Add the turnip, basil, garlic, greens, and the remaining ½ teaspoon salt. Cook for 3 minutes, stirring occasionally, then add the broccoli and cook for another 5 minutes.

4. Pour the egg mixture into the pan and dollop with the goat cheese. Transfer the pan to the oven and bake until the center is barely set, 20 to 22 minutes.

5. Let the frittata rest for 5 minutes, then top with a pile of microgreens. Slice the frittata and serve.

TIP: It's easy to keep the egg base of the frittata the same and mix up your veggies and cheese for different combinations.

YIELD: 8–10 SERVINGS PREP: 20 MIN COOK: 5 MIN

WHITE BEAN HUMMUS WITH WALNUT OIL

Creamy and light, this white bean hummus gets a lift from lemon and coriander, with a silky texture thanks to tahini and ice. The ice helps create an ultrasmooth blend, while a quick homemade walnut oil adds depth. Finished with fresh flat-leaf parsley, it's an aromatic rendition of a classic dip.

INGREDIENTS

WHITE BEAN HUMMUS

2 (15-ounce) cans great northern beans, drained, divided
¼ cup tahini
1 lemon, juiced
2 teaspoons kosher salt
2 teaspoons ground coriander
2 garlic cloves
3 to 4 ice cubes

TOASTED WALNUT OIL

1 tablespoon minced fresh flat-leaf parsley stems
½ cup walnut halves
⅓ cup extra-virgin olive oil
2 teaspoons whole cumin seeds
¼ cup fresh flat-leaf parsley leaves

DIRECTIONS

1. Reserve 2 tablespoons of the beans for presentation. To the bowl of a food processor, add the remaining beans, tahini, lemon juice, salt, and coriander. Grate or mince the garlic cloves and add them to the bowl. Process until the mixture looks smooth.

2. With the food processor still running, add the ice cubes one at a time. Process until the ice is fully incorporated and the hummus is light and smooth. Transfer the hummus to a bowl or plate.

3. Place the parsley stems in a medium heat-proof bowl. Set aside. Roughly chop the walnuts and add them to a small skillet along with the olive oil. Set over medium-low heat and watch closely. Once the oil begins to bubble around the walnuts, add the cumin seeds. Stir frequently until the walnuts smell fragrant and start to brown, 3 to 4 minutes.

4. Immediately remove from heat and pour the walnut oil over the parsley stems. At first the oil will rapidly bubble, but it will mellow after several seconds. Set aside to cool.

5. To serve, spoon the walnut oil over the plated hummus. Top with the reserved beans, then roughly chop the parsley leaves and sprinkle over the top.

TIP: Drizzle the toasted walnut oil over roasted carrots or parsnips for a simple, elevated side.

YIELD: 5 ½ CUPS PREP: 15 MIN COOK: 40 MIN REST: 30 MIN

LOADED EVERYDAY GRANOLA

I eat granola with yogurt every morning, and this homemade version is everything I want in a breakfast staple—crunchy, golden, and just sweet enough. Use the quantities as your guide and feel free to mix and match nuts according to your mood.

INGREDIENTS

1 cup old-fashioned rolled oats
½ cup pecan halves
½ cup hazelnuts
½ cup sliced almonds
½ cup pepitas
¼ cup sunflower seeds
½ cup unsweetened coconut flakes
½ cup wheat germ
½ teaspoon kosher salt
¼ cup virgin or refined coconut oil, melted
3 tablespoons honey
1 teaspoon vanilla extract
¾ cup golden raisins
½ cup chopped white chocolate

DIRECTIONS

1. Preheat the oven to 350 degrees. Add the oats to a large bowl. Chop the pecans and hazelnuts, then add them to the bowl along with the almonds, pepitas, sunflower seeds, coconut flakes, wheat germ, and salt. Toss to combine. Add the oil, honey, and vanilla. Stir until well combined, then transfer to an 18 x 13-inch sheet pan and spread evenly in a single layer.

2. Bake for 35 to 40 minutes, stirring every 10 minutes, until the granola is deeply golden and smells fragrant. Remove from the oven and cool completely to room temperature for at least 30 minutes.

3. Transfer the granola to a bowl and toss with the raisins and white chocolate. Store in an airtight container for 3 to 4 weeks. Serve over a bowl of yogurt with fresh fruit, jam, or fruit compote.

YIELD: 35 CROSTINI | PREP: 40 MIN | COOK: 14 MIN | REST: 1 HR

WHIPPED RICOTTA CROSTINI

These crostini are a simple, elegant appetizer that feeds a crowd. Using croissants in place of a typical baguette yields a supremely buttery toast that delicately shatters beneath each bite of cloudlike ricotta. For a little extra color, finish with flaky salt and a sprinkle of dried edible flowers.

INGREDIENTS

3 ½ cups (30 ounces) whole-milk ricotta
½ cup heavy whipping cream
1 teaspoon kosher salt
3 to 4 large croissants
2 tablespoons extra-virgin olive oil
Flaky salt, for serving
Dried edible flowers, for serving (optional)

DIRECTIONS

1. To the bowl of a stand mixer fitted with a whisk attachment, add the ricotta, cream, and salt. Whip on medium-high speed, scraping the sides of the bowl occasionally, for 3 to 4 minutes. The mixture will be light and fluffy.

2. Transfer the whipped ricotta to a piping bag or gallon storage bag and refrigerate for at least 1 hour, or up to overnight.

3. Preheat the oven to 375 degrees and slice the croissants into ½-inch slices, just like you would a loaf of bread, to yield about 10 slices per croissant. Nestle the slices onto a parchment-lined 18 x 13-inch sheet pan in a single layer, using two pans if needed.

4. Brush the croissants on both sides with the oil, then transfer to the oven and bake for 7 to 8 minutes. Flip the croissants, then bake for another 5 to 6 minutes until they are deeply toasted and crisp. Set aside to cool completely.

5. When ready to assemble, cut the tip of the bag to create a ¼-inch opening. Pipe the whipped ricotta onto each crostini in a squiggle motion, then sprinkle with flaky salt and dried flowers (if using). Serve immediately.

YIELD: 8 SERVINGS PREP: 30 MIN REST: 8 HR

NO-BAKE BAY LEAF CHEESECAKE

This no-bake cheesecake is inspired by a flavor combination I tried at Jeni's Splendid Ice Creams. With its infusion of bay leaves whipped into airy ricotta and cream cheese, this dessert is impressive yet deceptively simple to make.

INGREDIENTS

GRAHAM CRACKER CRUST

18 rectangular graham cracker sheets (280 grams)
½ cup (113 grams) unsalted butter, melted
½ teaspoon kosher salt

CHEESECAKE FILLING

¾ cup (150 grams) granulated sugar
5 medium dried bay leaves, plus more for presentation
2 (8-ounce) blocks (448 grams) full-fat cream cheese, room temperature
1 cup (227 grams) whole-milk ricotta, cold
1 teaspoon lemon juice
½ teaspoon kosher salt
1⅓ cups (303 grams) heavy whipping cream, cold
Orange marmalade, for serving (optional)

TIP: For an elevated presentation, add florals or fresh herbs around the base of the cheesecake.

DIRECTIONS

1. In a food processor, pulse the graham crackers into fine crumbs. Add the melted butter and salt, then pulse until the mixture resembles wet sand. Press the mixture very firmly into a 9-inch springform pan, making sure the crust extends 1 to 2 inches up the side of the pan. Refrigerate while preparing the cheesecake filling.

2. Wipe down the bowl of the food processor, then add the sugar and bay leaves. Process for 2 to 3 minutes until the bay leaves are ground and the sugar is ultrafine, almost resembling powdered sugar.

3. Add the bay leaf sugar and the cream cheese to the bowl of a stand mixer. Using a paddle attachment, beat on medium speed until smooth and airy, 3 to 4 minutes.

4. Thoroughly scrape the sides of the bowl and the paddle to ensure that everything is fully incorporated. Add the ricotta, lemon juice, and salt and beat on medium speed for another 2 to 3 minutes until well combined. Transfer the mixture to a large bowl and set aside.

5. Wash and dry the bowl of the stand mixer and switch to a whisk attachment. Add the cream and whip to stiff peaks. Gently fold the whipped cream into the cream cheese mixture until no streaks remain.

6. Transfer the cheesecake filling to the prepared crust, smoothing the top of the filling. If desired, top with a few whole bay leaves for presentation. Cover the pan tightly with plastic wrap and refrigerate for at least 8 hours or overnight. To serve, slice and top with a small spoonful of orange marmalade (if using).

YIELD: 8 DRINKS PREP: 10 MIN

ROSY MIMOSAS

A fluted glass of sunny, fizzy orange juice signals the start of a great breakfast. Swap the champagne for a fruitier sparkling rosé and add a drop of rose water for a hint of florals to round out a relaxed (yet polished) brunch.

INGREDIENTS

2 cups freshly squeezed orange juice (7 to 8 navel oranges)
¼ teaspoon rose water
¼ teaspoon kosher salt
40 ounces sparkling rosé wine (about 1½ 750-mL bottles)

DIRECTIONS

1. To a small pitcher or jar, add the orange juice, rose water, and salt, and stir to combine. Chill until ready to serve.
2. Divide the orange juice between 8 champagne glasses, adding about 2 ounces to each. Just before serving, top each glass with about 5 ounces of sparkling rosé.

TIP: To make this mimosa into a mocktail, swap sparkling rosé with your favorite sparkling cider.

FARMERS MARKET LUNCH

ON THE MENU

WHOLE WHEAT FOCACCIA

MARKET BLTA

STRAWBERRY TABBOULEH

TZATZIKI CUCUMBERS

SHEA'S FAVORITE CHOCOLATE CHIP COOKIE

Walking through a farmers market without a plan and letting the ingredients guide me is the only kind of thrill I'm after these days. I love filling a bag with juicy heirloom tomatoes, plump strawberries, crisp cucumbers, and a bunch of herbs, and heading home to figure out the rest. This lunch menu was born from one of those unhurried mornings. It's veggie forward, unfussy, and full of flavor. Homemade whole wheat focaccia sets the stage for a BLTA layered with sun-ripened tomatoes, basil and lemon-pepper mayo, and crispy bacon. A twist on traditional tabbouleh brings berries into the mix for something unexpected and bright. Tzatziki cucumbers offer a light contrast, perfect for scooping straight from the bowl. For a sweet treat, my all-time favorite dessert is on the menu—a perfectly chewy, melty, just-salty-enough chocolate chip cookie.

This is the kind of lunch you throw together barefoot in the kitchen, windows open, produce piled high on the counter. It's casual and relaxed, but made with care—and that, to me, is the essence of a perfect afternoon.

STYLING: *I always incorporate at least one item with a woven texture to break up the glossy ceramics and add an organic touch.*

YIELD: 1 LOAF PREP: 50 MIN REST: 2 HR COOK: 30 MIN

WHOLE WHEAT FOCACCIA

This focaccia is ideal for beginners and seasoned bakers alike. Thanks to a high hydration percentage, it yields a surprisingly chewy, bubbly texture in only a few hours. Whether you enjoy it plain or piled high for a sandwich, its plush crumb will keep you coming back for more.

INGREDIENTS

4 cups (520 grams) bread flour, fluffed, scooped, and leveled
2 ¼ cups (293 grams) whole wheat flour, fluffed, scooped, and leveled
5 teaspoons (18 grams) kosher salt
2 teaspoons fast-rising instant yeast
3 ⅓ cups (770 grams) water
½ cup (100 grams) extra-virgin olive oil, divided
Unsalted butter, for greasing pan
Flaky salt or coarse gray French salt

DIRECTIONS

1. In the bowl of a stand mixer, whisk together the bread flour, whole wheat flour, salt, and yeast. Warm the water to 105 to 110 degrees, then add it to the flour mixture.

2. Mix with a bread hook on medium speed for 2 to 3 minutes, until the flour and water are combined, scraping the sides and bottom of the bowl about halfway through to make sure the flour is completely incorporated. The dough will look very slack and wet.

3. Increase the speed of the mixer to medium-high and continue mixing for 15 to 20 minutes, or until the dough pulls away completely from the sides and bottom of the bowl and clings to the bread hook. The dough pulling away from the bowl is more important than the exact mixing time.

4. Add ¼ cup (50 grams) of the oil to your largest bowl and turn it to coat the sides. Use a rubber spatula to help you transfer the dough to the bowl, as the dough will still be sticky. With oiled hands, gently stretch the dough from the center about 12 inches out of the bowl, then lower it back to the bowl. Rotate the bowl 90 degrees and repeat the process three more times.

5. Cover the bowl with plastic wrap or a linen towel and let the dough rise until at least doubled, about 1 hour. You'll know it's ready when you gently press the dough with a finger and the indent slowly springs back.

6. Generously grease an 18 x 13-inch sheet pan with butter, then add the remaining ¼ cup (50 grams) oil. Transfer the risen dough onto the sheet pan and gently stretch it to fill the pan. If it doesn't extend to all corners and sides perfectly, that's okay. The second rise will fill in the gaps.

Continued on next page →

7. Lightly cover the pan with plastic wrap and set aside to rise until it passes the finger test again, about 45 minutes to 1 hour. Meanwhile, preheat the oven to 450 degrees.

8. Once risen, use your fingers to thoroughly dimple the dough. Make your hands into a claw shape and press firmly into the springy dough to create indentations all over. Leave any big bubbles intact. Sprinkle the dough with flaky or coarse gray salt.

9. Bake for 25 to 30 minutes, or until the top of the focaccia is deep brown and sounds hollow when tapped. If using a meat thermometer, the internal temperature of the dough will read 185 to 190 degrees. Wait for the bread to cool (or don't), then slice it up and enjoy.

YIELD: 6 SANDWICHES PREP: 25 MIN COOK: 27 MIN

MARKET BLTA

While the premise of a BLTA is simple, a good spread and salty tomatoes will take your sandwich game to the next level. This BLTA features basil and lemon-pepper mayo, a fresh, zesty spread you'll want to slather on every sandwich from here on out.

INGREDIENTS

BASIL & LEMON-PEPPER MAYO

1 lemon
1 cup fresh basil leaves, tightly packed
½ cup mayonnaise
1 teaspoon freshly cracked black pepper
¼ teaspoon kosher salt

SANDWICH ASSEMBLY

15 thick-cut slices applewood smoked bacon
½ loaf Whole Wheat Focaccia (pg. 53), or store-bought focaccia
2 heirloom tomatoes
1 teaspoon kosher salt
1 medium head romaine, leaves removed
3 avocados

DIRECTIONS

1. Zest the lemon and measure 2 teaspoons of zest. Make the basil and lemon-pepper mayo by adding the basil, mayonnaise, lemon zest, pepper, and salt to a food processor and blending to combine. Store in an airtight container in the fridge until ready to use.

2. Preheat the oven to 375 degrees and top an 18 x 13-inch sheet pan with a cooling rack or parchment paper. Cut each slice of bacon in half crosswise and lay them on the pan. Bake in the lower third of the oven for 18 to 22 minutes, or until the fat has rendered and the bacon is crisp and golden.

3. While the bacon cooks, slice the loaf of focaccia into 4 x 4-inch squares, then slice each square horizontally down the center to create a top and bottom slice. If desired, toast the focaccia pieces, interior side facing up, in the top rack of the oven above the bacon. Toast for about 5 minutes, or to your liking.

4. Slice the heirloom tomatoes into ¼- to ½-inch slices, depending on your preference. Lay each slice on a paper towel and sprinkle with the salt. Let rest while preparing the rest of the sandwich.

5. Wash the romaine leaves and pat them dry. Finally, slice the avocados.

6. To assemble, add a few leaves of romaine to the bottom slice of bread and slather the top slice with a generous amount of the basil and lemon pepper mayo. Pat a tomato slice dry and place atop the lettuce, add a few slices of avocado, and stack with five strips of bacon. Add the top slice of bread, slice in half, and enjoy.

YIELD: 6–8 SERVINGS PREP: 30 MIN REST: 1 HR

STRAWBERRY TABBOULEH

This colorful, herb-packed strawberry tabbouleh is a nontraditional take on the classic, with ripe berries, sliced almonds, and salty feta in every bite. It's a brilliant salad that balances sweet, savory, and citrusy flavors—a playful side dish for spring gatherings or an easy lunch upgrade.

INGREDIENTS

½ cup coarse red bulgur wheat
½ cup boiling water
1 pound fresh strawberries
1 bunch fresh flat-leaf parsley
1 cup fresh mint leaves, loosely packed
3 green onions
⅔ cup sliced almonds
2 lemons
½ teaspoon freshly cracked black pepper
1 teaspoon kosher salt
½ teaspoon ground sumac
3 tablespoons extra-virgin olive oil
1 (4-ounce) block feta

DIRECTIONS

1. Soak the red bulgur in a large heat-proof bowl with the boiling water for 45 minutes to 1 hour, uncovered. Fluff the bulgur with a fork.

2. Hull and dice the strawberries, then add them to the bulgur. Using only one or two passes of the knife, mince the parsley bunch (including the tender stems) and mint leaves, then thinly slice the green parts of the green onion. Don't chop the herbs any more than you have to—this allows them to retain their volume and prevents bruising the leaves. Add the minced herbs and sliced almonds to the bulgur.

3. Juice the lemons and measure ⅓ cup lemon juice, then add the juice to the tabbouleh along with the pepper, salt, and sumac. Finally, add the olive oil and toss to combine. Crumble the feta over the salad and toss once more. Serve immediately.

YIELD: 6 SERVINGS PREP: 20 MIN

TZATZIKI CUCUMBERS

Thanks to a punchy dill vinaigrette and creamy yogurt base, these tzatziki-inspired cucumbers are cool, crunchy, and packed with flavor. With just a few ingredients and simple prep, this dish delivers the refreshing bite of tzatziki in an engaging, deconstructed form.

INGREDIENTS

- ⅓ cup extra-virgin olive oil
- 1 tablespoon toasted sesame seeds
- ½ teaspoon granulated sugar
- ¾ teaspoon kosher salt, divided
- ¼ cup fresh dill, packed
- 1 garlic clove
- 1 lemon
- 2 English cucumbers
- ¾ cup whole-milk plain Greek yogurt

DIRECTIONS

1. In a large bowl make the vinaigrette by whisking together the oil, sesame seeds, sugar, and ½ teaspoon of the salt. Chop the dill, grate or finely mince the garlic, and zest and juice the lemon. Add the dill, garlic, lemon zest, and lemon juice to the oil and whisk to combine.

2. Cut the cucumbers into thirds crosswise, then smash each piece with the side of the knife or a mallet. Roughly chop the smashed cucumbers and add them to the vinaigrette. Stir to combine.

3. Add the remaining ¼ teaspoon salt to the yogurt and stir to combine. Spread the yogurt over the bottom of a serving platter or shallow bowl, then spoon the cucumbers on top of the yogurt. Pour any remaining vinaigrette over the top and serve.

YIELD: 20–22 COOKIES PREP: 25 MIN COOK: 12 MIN

SHEA'S FAVORITE CHOCOLATE CHIP COOKIE

I've baked more chocolate chip cookies than I can count, with hundreds of batches forged from a lifelong love of warm, melty dough. This recipe combines all my favorites—crisp edges, puddles of chocolate, and just the right hint of salt—without any fuss or complicated steps.

INGREDIENTS

1 cup (226 grams) unsalted butter, slightly softened
1 cup (213 grams) firmly packed light brown sugar
¾ cup (149 grams) granulated sugar
1 tablespoon (14 grams) vanilla extract
2 eggs, cold
3 ¼ cups (423 grams) all-purpose flour, fluffed, scooped, and leveled
2 teaspoons baking powder
1 teaspoon baking soda
1½ teaspoons kosher salt
1¼ cups (213 grams) chopped 70% dark chocolate
1½ cups (255 grams) semisweet chocolate chips
Flaky salt, for serving

DIRECTIONS

1. Preheat the oven to 375 degrees. In a stand mixer fitted with a paddle attachment, cream the butter, brown sugar, and granulated sugar for 5 minutes, scraping the sides of the bowl and the paddle about halfway through.

2. Add the vanilla and then the eggs one at a time, beating for 30 seconds on medium speed between each addition. Thoroughly scrape the the sides of the bowl and the paddle, mixing for another 10 to 15 seconds to incorporate any dense bits of butter and sugar.

3. To a medium bowl, add the flour, baking powder, baking soda, and salt and whisk to combine. Add the flour mixture, chopped chocolate, and chocolate chips to the stand mixer. Pulse the mixer a few times to begin incorporating the flour. Slowly increase the speed to medium and mix for 30 seconds to 1 minute until no floury spots remain.

4. Using a large ¼-cup (60-gram) cookie scoop, scoop the dough into balls and place 2 inches apart on a parchment-lined baking sheet. Bake for 10 to 12 minutes, or until golden at the edges. Sprinkle with flaky salt and enjoy.

TIP: Store dough balls in the freezer for up to 3 months. Preheat the oven to 350 degrees and bake the frozen cookie dough for 14 to 15 minutes.

CELEBRATION DINNER

ON THE MENU

TENDER GRILLED FLANK STEAK

FARRO ARUGULA SALAD

CONFETTI BIRTHDAY BLONDIES

In our home, momentous occasions (both big and small) are marked with what I like to call a "medium fancy" dinner. It's not a formal affair, but it's more than your everyday meal. Whether we're ringing in a birthday, celebrating the end of a school year, or gathering simply because the moment is worth honoring, a prepared dinner sets the tone. The ritual of planning a menu and setting the table has a way of making the guest of honor feel seen and appreciated. As I do in my interior design process, I create tablescapes using a colorful or textural detail as a jumping-off point. Inspired by the playful palette of sprinkles in the blondies, I opted to set a neutral foundation in the linens to allow the vibrant florals to be the center of attention.

Layered between flower arrangements is a colorful, crowd-pleasing menu that balances depth and vibrance with a celebratory finish. Flank steak is grilled until charred and juicy, then finished with a spoonful of cool crème fraîche and lime zest for a bright, unexpected twist. It's anchored by a hearty farro arugula salad, which is packed with texture from candied almonds and shavings of Manchego. Lastly, no celebration is complete without confetti. Confetti blondies, baked golden and dotted with sprinkles, channel the spirit of a birthday cake in one chewy bite—no cake decorating required.

STYLING: *A bar cart is a handy entertaining tool that can be moved around indoors and out to provide an additional surface for serving.*

TENDER GRILLED FLANK STEAK

This flank steak delivers bold flavor with minimal effort. It's grilled to achieve a caramelized crust, then finished with a generous dollop of crème fraîche and lime. A few smart techniques, like pounding the meat and applying a well-balanced spice rub, make it surprisingly tender and anything but ordinary.

INGREDIENTS

1 tablespoon freshly cracked black pepper, plus more for serving
1 tablespoon ground mustard powder
1 teaspoon ground cumin
¾ teaspoon baking soda
3 ½ teaspoons kosher salt, divided
2 pounds flank steak
1 cup crème fraîche
2 tablespoons neutral oil, such as avocado oil
1 lime

DIRECTIONS

1. In a small bowl combine the pepper, mustard powder, cumin, baking soda, and 3 teaspoons of the salt.

2. Pat the flank steak dry, then set it on a cutting board and cover with plastic wrap. Pound the steak until it's no more than ¾ inch thick. Discard the plastic wrap. Rub all of the seasoning blend over both sides of the steak. Let the steak sit at room temperature for 30 minutes.

3. Meanwhile, whisk together the crème fraîche and the remaining ½ teaspoon salt. Refrigerate until ready to serve.

4. Preheat the grill to 350 degrees over medium heat. Gently pat the steak dry again, then rub 1 tablespoon oil on each side.

5. Once the grill is hot, sear the steak for 5 to 6 minutes. Flip and sear for another 4 to 5 minutes, or until the internal temperature reaches 135 degrees for a medium-rare steak. Transfer the steak to a cutting board and let it rest for 10 minutes.

6. To serve, slice the steak against the grain. Spoon the crème fraîche over the top and add more black pepper. Zest the lime over the top to taste. Finally, cut the lime into wedges and squeeze them over the steak before serving.

YIELD: 6 SERVINGS PREP: 10 MIN COOK: 35 MIN

FARRO ARUGULA SALAD

This make-ahead arugula salad is a multitextured, satiating mix that is just as fitting for a celebration as for a weekday lunch. Do yourself a kindness and make a double batch of the candied almonds in step 3—they are addictive.

INGREDIENTS

SALAD & ASSEMBLY

1 tablespoon kosher salt
½ cup farro, rinsed
½ cup black or French green lentils, rinsed
1 cup sliced almonds
2 tablespoons unsalted butter
3 tablespoons firmly packed light brown sugar
1 teaspoon ground coriander
1 tablespoon water
5 ounces arugula
3 ounces Manchego

FIG VINAIGRETTE

2 lemons
½ cup neutral oil, such as avocado oil
¼ cup fig preserves
¾ teaspoon kosher salt
1 garlic clove

TIP: To make ahead of time, toss the farro, lentils, arugula, and shaved Manchego together and store in an airtight container in the fridge. Keep the vinaigrette in the fridge and the candied nuts at room temperature, then assemble when ready to eat.

DIRECTIONS

1. Add 2 quarts water to a large, heavy-bottomed Dutch oven. Add the salt, then bring to a boil. Add the rinsed farro and boil, stirring occasionally, for 10 minutes.

2. Add the lentils to the pot with the farro and continue cooking for another 15 to 20 minutes, or until both the lentils and farro are tender but still firm. Drain, then allow the farro and lentils to cool completely by transferring them to an 18 x 13-inch sheet pan and spreading in a single layer.

3. While the grains cool, heat a skillet over medium-low heat and add the sliced almonds, butter, brown sugar, and coriander. Once the butter is melted, add the water and cook for another 3 to 4 minutes, stirring constantly. The nuts will smell aromatic, and the sugar mixture will become sticky. Transfer the nuts to a plate to cool.

4. Make the vinaigrette by juicing the lemon and measuring ¼ cup juice. Add the lemon juice, oil, fig preserves, and salt to a small bowl. Grate in the garlic clove, then whisk to combine.

5. To assemble the salad, toss the farro, lentils, and arugula together in a large bowl. Dress the salad in the vinaigrette to taste, then shave the Manchego over the top and finish with the candied almonds.

YIELD: 9 BARS | PREP: 15 MIN | COOK: 45 MIN | REST: 2 HR

CONFETTI BIRTHDAY BLONDIES

These confetti blondies are everything you want in a celebratory treat—chewy, sweet, and packed with buttery vanilla flavor, plus a festive pop of sprinkles in every bite. With a doughlike batter and no-fuss technique, they bake up thick and golden, perfect for slicing into party-ready squares.

INGREDIENTS

- ¾ cup (170 grams) unsalted butter, plus more for greasing the pan
- 1½ cups (320 grams) firmly packed light brown sugar
- ½ cup (60 grams) powdered sugar
- 2 teaspoons vanilla extract
- ¼ teaspoon almond extract
- 2 eggs
- 1 egg yolk
- 2¼ cups (293 grams) all-purpose flour, fluffed, scooped, and leveled
- 1 teaspoon baking powder
- 1¼ teaspoons kosher salt
- ¾ cup (135 grams) rainbow sprinkles

DIRECTIONS

1. Preheat the oven to 350 degrees. Lightly grease a 9 x 9-inch baking dish with butter, then line with parchment paper and set aside.

2. Add the brown sugar and powdered sugar to a stand mixer fitted with a paddle attachment. Melt ¾ cup of butter in a saucepan over medium heat, then add it to the stand mixer. Beat for about 2 minutes on medium speed, until the mixture resembles a grainy caramel. It will be somewhat separated.

3. Scrape the sides of the bowl and the paddle, then add the vanilla and almond extracts. Continue beating on medium-high speed for 2 to 3 minutes. Scrape the bowl once more and add the eggs and egg yolk, one at a time, beating for 20 to 30 seconds between each addition. Continue beating until the mixture is pale in color with an airy texture.

4. In a separate bowl whisk together the flour, baking powder, salt, and sprinkles. Remove the bowl from the stand mixer, then fold the flour mixture into the egg mixture using a rubber spatula until no dry streaks remain. The batter will be quite thick, almost like a dough.

5. Transfer the batter to the prepared baking dish, smoothing the top with the spatula. Bake for 38 to 45 minutes, or until an inserted toothpick comes out with a few moist crumbs. If using a metal pan, your bake time will be shorter. If using a glass or ceramic baking dish, your bake time will be longer.

6. As tempting as it is to cut into the blondies right after they come out of the oven, let them cool completely—about 2 hours. Once no trace of warmth remains, slice the blondies into squares and serve.

SPRING FÊTE

ON THE MENU

MELT-IN-YOUR-MOUTH SALMON WITH ASPARAGUS

LEMONY SMASHED POTATOES

BUTTER LETTUCE SALAD

BASIL GARLIC KNOTS

FOUR-LAYER SOUTHERN COCONUT CAKE

Designed for Easter dinner or a formal spring supper, this table is a commemoration of the season's gentle renewal. Here we layered the table with natural textures and botanical details, set against a palette of powdery blues and fresh grass greens. Sprigs of lilies of the valley arranged simply in silver vessels create an atmosphere that feels timeless yet uncomplicated.

The menu reflects that balance of beauty and ease—tender roasted salmon with asparagus on a single sheet pan, noteworthy enough for any celebration yet ready in under an hour. It's paired with smashed baby potatoes finished with lemon and herbs, and a delicate salad of butter lettuce, avocado, and springy snap peas. Warm basil garlic knots invite hands to reach and share. For dessert, a towering coconut cake, inspired by the classic Southern version I grew up loving, promises a sweet, unforgettable finish.

STYLING: *Skip the napkin ring and try ribbons or twine.*

YIELD: 6 SERVINGS PREP: 25 MIN COOK: 30 MIN

MELT-IN-YOUR-MOUTH SALMON WITH ASPARAGUS

This succulent salmon is topped with a fragrant compound butter, then gently roasted until it barely flakes apart. Cooked alongside al dente asparagus and a touch of lemon, it's a visual stunner that comes together quickly enough to serve at a formal party or on a weeknight.

INGREDIENTS

½ cup unsalted butter, softened
2 tablespoons honey
3 garlic cloves
1 small shallot
2 tablespoons fresh dill, plus more for serving
1-inch knob fresh ginger
3-pound slab Atlantic salmon, boneless and skinless
1½ pounds fresh asparagus
1 tablespoon kosher salt
1 lemon, for serving

DIRECTIONS

1. Preheat the oven to 325 degrees. To a small bowl add the butter and honey. Finely mince the garlic, shallot, and dill, then grate the ginger and add everything to the butter. Use a metal spoon to stir and mash the ingredients into a compound butter and set aside.

2. Pat the salmon dry and place on an 18 x 13-inch sheet pan. Nestle the asparagus next to the salmon—the sheet pan will be very full. Generously season the salmon filet with at least 2 teaspoons salt, then use the rest of the salt to season the asparagus.

3. Dollop all of the butter over the salmon. Bake the salmon and asparagus for 25 to 30 minutes, or until the internal temperature of the salmon reaches 135 to 140 degrees. The fish will flake apart effortlessly and look matte across the top.

4. Remove the salmon and asparagus from the oven and spread the aromatics left behind from the melted butter evenly over the fish. Transfer the salmon and asparagus to a platter. There will be a significant amount of butter left behind on the pan, which you can spoon over the salmon if you would like. Thinly slice the lemon, arrange the slices over the top of the salmon, and serve.

Microplane

YIELD: 8 SERVINGS PREP: 40 MIN COOK: 1 HR 10 MIN

LEMONY SMASHED POTATOES

Crispy yet fluffy, this is the ultimate combination of a fried potato and a mashed potato. Finished with a blanket of fresh Parmigiano-Reggiano and a flurry of herbs, it's a side that steals the spotlight. Plus, it's fun to make—let your kids help with the smashing.

INGREDIENTS

- 3 pounds baby Yukon Gold potatoes
- ⅓ cup kosher salt, plus more for serving
- 1 cup finely grated Parmigiano-Reggiano
- 1 lemon
- 4 tablespoons extra-virgin olive oil
- ½ cup assorted fresh herbs, such as dill, chives, mint, basil, or cilantro

DIRECTIONS

1. Place an 18 x 13-inch sheet pan in the oven and preheat to 400 degrees. Bring a large pot of water to a boil, then add the potatoes and salt. Boil for 20 to 25 minutes, until the potatoes are very tender and give no resistance when pierced with a fork. Drain and set aside to cool slightly.

2. Add the Parmigiano-Reggiano to a small bowl. Zest the lemon into the bowl and mix to combine. Using the bottom of a glass or measuring cup, gently smash each potato on a cutting board.

3. Remove the preheated pan from the oven and drizzle it with half of the oil. Set the potatoes on the pan and coat them with the remaining oil.

4. Sprinkle the Parmigiano-Reggiano and lemon zest all over the tops of the potatoes and transfer to the oven. Bake for 40 to 45 minutes, or until the edges and bottoms of the potatoes are golden.

5. Arrange the potatoes on a platter. Roughly chop the assorted herbs, then sprinkle them over the potatoes. Salt to taste and serve.

YIELD: 6 SERVINGS PREP: 25 MIN

BUTTER LETTUCE SALAD

This salad captures the essence of spring with supple butter lettuce, vibrant snap peas, and velvety avocado layered beneath a light buttermilk chive dressing. A final scatter of roasted sunflower seeds adds just enough crunch.

INGREDIENTS

BUTTERMILK CHIVE DRESSING

½ cup buttermilk
2 tablespoons sour cream
1 tablespoon lemon juice
½ teaspoon kosher salt
½ cup minced fresh chives

SALAD & ASSEMBLY

1 head butter lettuce
¼ pound snap peas
1 avocado
2 tablespoons roasted sunflower seeds

DIRECTIONS

1. To make the dressing add the buttermilk, sour cream, lemon juice, salt, and chives to a jar or bowl and whisk to combine. Refrigerate until ready to use.

2. Gently pull the leaves off the head of butter lettuce, then wash them and pat them dry. Arrange the leaves in a bowl or on a platter. Halve the snap peas by slicing them down the center seam, then slice the avocado. Arrange the peas and avocado over the lettuce.

3. Just before serving, drizzle the salad with the dressing and sprinkle with the sunflower seeds.

YIELD: 36 ROLLS | PREP: 45 MIN | REST: 1 HR 30 MIN | COOK: 16 MIN

BASIL GARLIC KNOTS

These basil garlic knots are soft and fragrant, with fresh basil and garlic worked right into the dough and brushed on top for double the impact. Baked until barely browned and finished with a buttery gloss, they have a way of disappearing before the meal even begins.

INGREDIENTS

4 garlic cloves, divided
½ cup fresh basil leaves, packed, divided
1 recipe All-Purpose Dough (pg. 187)
4 tablespoons unsalted butter
1 teaspoon kosher salt

DIRECTIONS

1. Finely mince the garlic and chop the basil. Prepare the All-Purpose Dough (pg. 187) through step 4, adding half of the garlic and basil to the dough along with the warm milk and water in step 2.

2. Line two 18 x 13-inch sheet pans with parchment paper. Dust the counter with flour and use a spatula to coax the dough onto the work surface. Lightly dust the top of the dough with flour, then roll the dough into a 15 x 18-inch rectangle. Use a pizza cutter to slice the dough in half lengthwise, then slice the dough into 1-inch strips following the long edge.

3. Preheat the oven to 400 degrees. Tie each strip into a knot, tucking the long edges underneath, and place on the sheet pans about 2 inches apart. Cover the pans loosely with plastic wrap and let rise for another 20 to 30 minutes, until puffed but not quite doubled.

4. Melt the butter and add the salt and the remaining garlic and basil. Stir to combine and brush the tops of the rolls with the butter. There should be a fair amount of butter remaining. Bake the rolls for 12 to 16 minutes, rotating the pans about halfway through, until the tops are golden brown.

5. As soon as the rolls are finished baking, brush them with the remaining garlic butter and serve.

YIELD: 12 SERVINGS | PREP: 45 MIN | COOK: 35 MIN | REST: 2 HR

FOUR-LAYER SOUTHERN COCONUT CAKE

When I was growing up, there was a coconut cake on the table every Easter. This version gives you plenty of bang for your buck—just bake two layers, then slice in half horizontally to create an impressive centerpiece with an optimal cake-to-frosting ratio.

INGREDIENTS

COCONUT CAKE

- 6 egg whites
- 1½ cups (297 grams) granulated sugar, divided
- 2½ cups (325 grams) cake flour, fluffed, scooped, and leveled
- ⅓ cup (50 grams) coconut cream pudding mix
- 1 teaspoon kosher salt
- 2 teaspoons baking powder
- ¼ teaspoon baking soda
- ⅔ cup (150 grams) virgin coconut oil, melted
- ¾ cup (170 grams) sour cream
- 1¼ cups (301 grams) full-fat coconut milk
- ⅛ teaspoon coconut extract

COCONUT CREAM CHEESE FROSTING & ASSEMBLY

- 1 cup (226 grams) unsalted butter, room temperature
- 1 (8-ounce) block (224 grams) full-fat cream cheese, room temperature
- 3½ cups (420 grams) powdered sugar
- ½ teaspoon kosher salt
- 3 tablespoons (30 grams) coconut cream pudding mix
- 2 tablespoons (30 grams) full-fat coconut milk
- ¼ teaspoon coconut extract
- 4 cups (340 grams) sweetened coconut flakes

DIRECTIONS

Make the Cake

1. Preheat the oven to 350 degrees. Grease the bottom and sides of two 8-inch cake pans with butter. Line the bottom of each greased cake pan with a round of parchment paper and set aside.

2. Add the egg whites to the bowl of a stand mixer fitted with a whisk attachment. Whip the egg whites on medium speed for 9 to 10 minutes until stiff peaks form, slowly adding ¾ cup (149 grams) of the sugar as it whips. Transfer the whipped egg whites to a separate bowl.

3. Wash and dry the bowl of the stand mixer, then add the flour, pudding mix, salt, baking powder, baking soda, and the remaining ¾ cup (149 grams) sugar. Quickly whisk by hand to combine.

4. Fit the mixer with a paddle attachment and add the coconut oil to the flour mixture. Mix on medium speed for 30 seconds to 1 minute, until the mixture looks crumbly. Add the sour cream and mix for another 30 seconds. The batter will look like a wet biscuit dough.

5. Finally, add the coconut milk and coconut extract and mix for another 1 to 2 minutes on medium speed until the batter is silky. Gently fold half of the egg whites into the batter, then add the remaining egg whites and continue to fold until the batter is smooth but still aerated. Be careful not to overmix.

6. Divide the cake batter between the prepared pans. Bake for 32 to 35 minutes, or until the cake springs back when gently pressed and a toothpick comes out of the center with a few moist crumbs. Cool completely, then gently remove the cakes from their pans. The cakes will be very moist, so handle them with care.

Continued on next page →

Whip the Frosting

7. To a stand mixer fitted with a paddle attachment, add the butter and cream cheese. Whip on medium speed for 1 to 2 minutes, or until the mixture is fully combined and lighter in color.

8. Add the powdered sugar, salt, and pudding mix. Starting on low speed and increasing to medium speed, whip the frosting for 3 to 4 minutes until pale and aerated. Add the coconut milk and coconut extract, then whip for another 1 to 2 minutes. Refrigerate until ready to use, leaving the frosting at room temperature for about 1 hour before using.

Assemble

9. Slice each 8-inch cake round in half horizontally to create two layers. Apply a small dollop of frosting to the center of a cake stand and place the first cake round. Top the cake layer with a scant ½ cup frosting and ½ cup coconut flakes. Stack the next cake layer on top of the frosting, and continue frosting and adding the coconut flakes until all four layers are complete. The cake is extremely moist, so be gentle with the layers to avoid any breaks.

10. Frost the outside of the cake using the remaining frosting, then press the remaining coconut flakes around the cake. Slice and serve. Refrigerate any leftover cake in an airtight container or covered with plastic wrap. Bring to room temperature before serving.

SUMMER

ALFRESCO EVENING | BACKYARD BARBEQUE
CLASSIC SEAFOOD BOIL | PIZZA NIGHT | BEACH PICNIC

ALFRESCO EVENING

ON THE MENU

CAST-IRON PICCATA

GARDEN COUSCOUS SALAD

APPLE & BRIE BITES

BAGUETTE WITH BALSAMIC DIPPING OIL

LEMON BERRY PAVLOVA

Inspired by my love of Mediterranean living, this dinner celebrates the beauty of gathering outdoors with a table dressed in white, loosely arranged florals, and candles flickering as the sun sets. With a relaxed atmosphere, each detail sets the scene for food, conversation, and the evening itself to unfold naturally. The Mediterranean has taught me that elegance doesn't mean complication; it's about using simple, honest ingredients and creating an ambience that evokes wonder but never overwhelms.

The menu features cast-iron chicken piccata blanketed in a vibrant citrus sauce, accompanied by a couscous salad tossed with fresh herbs, crunchy pistachios, and briny olives. Crisp apple and Brie bites wrapped delicately in prosciutto add a savory-sweet balance, and slices of rustic baguette with balsamic dipping oil invite guests to slow down and delight in the occasion. To close the evening, individual lemon berry pavlovas are topped with mint for a fresh, airy finish. This is the dinner I serve when I want to make an evening feel memorable, warm, and refined. In all transparency, this is the dinner I make when I want to impress people.

STYLING: *Mix and match vintage plates in a similar color palette for a collected and considered look.*

YIELD: 6 SERVINGS PREP: 30 MIN COOK: 50 MIN

CAST-IRON PICCATA

Perhaps the juiciest chicken you'll ever make, this dish is easy to prepare and impressive to serve. A citrusy pan sauce of fresh orange and briny capers drapes over the bronzed bone-in, skin-on chicken breasts like a cashmere throw, effortlessly cutting through the richness.

INGREDIENTS

6 chicken breasts, bone-in and skin-on (about 6 pounds)
3 tablespoons kosher salt
4 ½ teaspoons freshly cracked black pepper
3 tablespoons neutral oil, such as avocado oil
5 garlic cloves
5 tablespoons capers, drained
¾ cup unsalted butter
1 navel orange

DIRECTIONS

1. Preheat the oven to 375 degrees. Liberally season each chicken breast with the salt and pepper, sprinkling them evenly over both sides. Let the chicken rest at room temperature for 20 to 25 minutes.

2. Pat the chicken breasts dry. Warm the oil in a 12- or 13-inch cast-iron skillet over medium-high heat until the oil ripples. Reduce the heat to medium, then place the chicken skin-side down in the hot pan, working in batches as needed. Place a weight, such as another heavy pan, on top of the chicken to press the skin into the hot pan. Let cook, undisturbed, for 3 to 5 minutes or until the chicken skin is deeply bronzed.

3. Remove the weight, flip the chicken skin-side up, and add the rest of the seared chicken back to the pan if you worked in batches. Transfer the pan to the oven and bake for 35 to 40 minutes, or until the internal temperature of the chicken registers 165 degrees.

4. While the chicken roasts, smash and peel the garlic cloves and set aside with the capers. Slice the butter into pieces, then juice the orange.

5. To make the sauce, transfer the chicken to a serving platter, leaving behind the drippings, and immediately place the pan over medium-low heat. Add the garlic, capers, and sliced butter to the pan. Once the butter is melted, slowly pour the orange juice into the pan, whisking constantly. Bring the sauce to a low simmer and cook for 3 to 4 minutes, stirring frequently, until slightly thickened and reduced.

6. Pour the pan sauce over the chicken breasts and serve.

YIELD: 8 SERVINGS PREP: 15 MIN COOK: 15 MIN

GARDEN COUSCOUS SALAD

This salad embodies my flavor palette—fresh, with ingredients that taste like they're plucked straight from the garden. It's a colorful mix of pistachios, red onion, and cucumber tossed with salty mizithra and couscous for a salad equally as good for lunch as for a dinner party.

INGREDIENTS

2 cups water
2 ¼ teaspoons kosher salt, divided
1 ½ cups pearl couscous
½ English cucumber
½ small red onion
½ cup fresh flat-leaf parsley, loosely packed
¼ cup fresh dill, loosely packed
¼ cup fresh mint leaves, loosely packed
⅓ cup roasted pistachios
⅓ cup kalamata olives, drained
1 cup grated mizithra
2 tablespoons champagne vinegar
4 tablespoons extra-virgin olive oil

DIRECTIONS

1. In a medium pot add the water and 2 teaspoons of the salt and bring to a boil. Add the pearl couscous and reduce the heat to low. Cover and cook for 13 to 14 minutes until the couscous is tender, stirring occasionally. Drain the couscous and rinse under cold water, then set aside.

2. Cut the cucumber into quarters lengthwise and thinly slice, then dice the onion. Add the onion to a sieve and rinse under cold water to cut its sharpness. Finely chop the parsley, dill, and mint, roughly chop the pistachios, and halve the olives down the center lengthwise.

3. Add the cooled couscous, cucumber, onion, parsley, dill, mint, pistachios, and olives to a large bowl. Add the cheese to the salad and toss.

4. Season the salad with the remaining ¼ teaspoon salt, vinegar, and oil. Toss once more to combine, then serve.

TIP: If you can't find mizithra at your cheese counter, feta or ricotta salata are great substitutes.

YIELD: 16–20 BUNDLES PREP: 20 MIN

APPLE & BRIE BITES

Every event needs a quick appetizer that's more assembly than cooking. These bites fit the bill. The apple is crisp and sweet, paired with creamy Brie and salty prosciutto. Topped with a drizzle of honey and a little flaky salt, it's a near-flawless starter.

INGREDIENTS

2 medium apples, such as Gala or Honeycrisp
8 ounces double-crème Brie
10 slices prosciutto
1 bunch fresh basil leaves
Honey and flaky salt, for serving

DIRECTIONS

1. Core and slice the apples, yielding 8 to 10 slices per apple.
2. Thinly slice the Brie into ¼-inch wide strips, halving them crosswise as needed to make 16 to 20 slices approximately 3 inches long.
3. Place a piece of Brie on top of the apple slice, then add a basil leaf. Tear the prosciutto in half crosswise and wrap the apple and Brie with one half of the prosciutto. Repeat with all remaining apple slices. Secure with a toothpick or skewer, if desired.
4. Arrange the bites on a serving platter. Drizzle with honey, sprinkle with flaky salt, and serve.

TIP: If preparing in advance, toss the apple slices in cold water, then pat dry and continue assembling. This will prevent the apples from browning.

YIELD: 6 SERVINGS PREP: 10 MIN

BAGUETTE WITH BALSAMIC DIPPING OIL

Crusty bread meets a pool of olive oil and balsamic topped with garden-fresh basil and thyme—a beautiful stir-and-serve starter that doubles as a centerpiece.

INGREDIENTS

⅓ cup extra-virgin olive oil
3 tablespoons balsamic vinegar
1 teaspoon red pepper flakes
½ teaspoon kosher salt
1 garlic clove
½ shallot
1 teaspoon minced fresh thyme leaves
1 tablespoon minced fresh basil leaves
1 French baguette

DIRECTIONS

1. Add the oil, vinegar, red pepper flakes, and salt to a shallow bowl or plate. Grate or finely mince the garlic clove and shallot.

2. Add the garlic, shallot, thyme, and basil to the oil mixture. Serve as is or use a fork to mix. Serve with torn or sliced pieces of bread and enjoy.

YIELD: 10 SERVINGS | PREP: 55 MIN | COOK: 1 HR 25 MIN | REST: 6 HR

LEMON BERRY PAVLOVA

This is an ode to my English neighbor, who generously delivers pavlova to celebrate big milestones. Taking cues from her berry-topped dessert, these individual servings are light and chewy, with an olive oil lemon curd that even a novice cook can whip together confidently.

INGREDIENTS

OLIVE OIL LEMON CURD

6 lemons
3 egg yolks, egg whites reserved for pavlova
1 whole egg
1 cup (198 grams) granulated sugar
½ teaspoon kosher salt
⅔ cup (133 grams) extra-virgin olive oil

PAVLOVA

4 egg whites (3 reserved from lemon curd)
¼ teaspoon kosher salt
¼ teaspoon cream of tartar
¼ teaspoon white vinegar
1 cup (198 grams) granulated sugar
1 pint blueberries and/or blackberries, for serving
Fresh mint leaves, for serving

TIP: Pavlova is the perfect blank canvas—pile high with fresh whipped cream and whatever fruit is in season.

DIRECTIONS

Make the Lemon Curd

1. Zest 1 lemon and collect 1 tablespoon of zest. Then juice all 6 lemons and collect ¾ cup (170 grams) of juice. To a blender, add the egg yolks, whole egg, lemon zest, lemon juice, sugar, and salt. Blend until smooth, about 30 seconds. With the blender running on medium-low speed, slowly add the olive oil, pouring it in a thin stream. Continue blending for another 30 seconds.

2. Pour the mixture into a saucepan and place over medium heat. Whisking constantly, cook the curd until it is thickened, with a slightly gelatinous texture that coats the back of a metal spoon, 6 to 10 minutes. Remove from heat, then store in an air-tight container in the fridge. Chill for at least 6 hours or overnight before using.

Make the Pavlova

3. Preheat the oven to 250 degrees. Add the egg whites to a stand mixer fitted with a whisk attachment. Beat for about 4 minutes on medium-high speed until the egg whites are frothy, whipped, and voluminous. Add the salt, cream of tartar, and vinegar and Briefly mix to combine. Gradually add the sugar about ¼ cup (50 grams) at a time, beating on medium speed for 60 seconds between each addition.

4. Once all the sugar is incorporated and the egg whites are glossy and reflective, continue whisking on medium-high speed for 15 to 17 minutes until stiff peaks form.

5. Line an 18 x 13-inch sheet pan with parchment paper. Using a ¼-cup capacity cookie scoop, dollop two scoops directly on top of one another to create a single pavlova. Alternatively, you can use one ½-cup measuring cup. Continue until there is no more meringue, placing each pavlova mound about 2 inches apart on

Continued on next page →

the pan. This will make 8 to 10 pavlovas. If needed, use a second sheet pan and bake both sheets simultaneously.

6. Using a spoon, push directly into the center of each pavlova mound and shape a deep well. Place the pavlovas into the oven, then immediately turn the temperature down to 200 degrees. Bake for 70 to 75 minutes, or until the pavlovas are set and no longer tacky but not yet crisp.

7. Leave the pavlovas in the oven and turn off the heat. Allow them to cool for at least 6 hours (for a chewier pavlova), or up to overnight (for a crisper pavlova). To serve, dollop each pavlova with a generous amount of lemon curd and top with the berries and mint leaves. Enjoy immediately.

TO MAKE A SINGLE, LARGE PAVLOVA

1. Follow the instructions through step 4. Line an 18 x 13-inch sheet pan with parchment paper and draw an 8-inch circle in the center. Flip the parchment paper over so you can still see the circle, but the ink is facing down.

2. Dollop all of the meringue in the center of the circle and use a spatula to spread the meringue to the edges. Create a shallow well in the center of the pavlova, leaving its edges about 2 ½ inches high.

3. Transfer to the oven and bake at 250 degrees for the first 15 minutes, then reduce the heat to 200 degrees. Continue baking for another 1 hour 45 minutes, until the pavlova is set and no longer tacky but not yet crisp.

4. Leave the pavlova in the oven and turn off the heat. Allow the pavlova to cool for at least 6 hours (for a chewier pavlova), or up to overnight (for a crisper pavlova). To serve, dollop the lemon curd in the center and top with the berries and mint leaves.

BACKYARD BARBEQUE

ON THE MENU

SYD'S SLIDERS FOR A CROWD

GRILLED SQUASH WITH WHIPPED FETA

CHARRED CORN SALAD WITH CILANTRO DRESSING

GRANDMA GLO'S COLA CAKE

WATERMELON RANCH WATER

Most summer meals at our house usually involve Syd at the grill and me pulling together the sides. It's a rhythm we've settled into easily over the years. I love it when entertaining feels like a true team effort, with everyone contributing something to the table. This menu is our take on a classic backyard barbeque with all our tried-and-true favorites. They're familiar and comforting, with a few refined touches tucked in—grilled squash over whipped feta, charred corn salad drizzled with cilantro dressing, Syd's famous sliders stacked high and ready for grabbing. Somewhere in the background, you can hear the splash of the pool and smell the smoky scent of the grill drifting through the air. These are the kinds of afternoons that feel both fleeting and slow all at once.

My birthday falls right in the heart of summer, and this is the menu I ask for year after year. It's not complete without a slice of my Grandma Glo's Cola Cake, supremely moist and blanketed by a layer of glossy chocolate frosting. One bite, and it's like time folds in on itself—part tradition, part celebration, and all heart.

STYLING: *Not every event requires formal place settings. I like to use a caddy to keep utensils organized and easy to reach.*

YIELD: 12 SLIDERS PREP: 45 MIN COOK: 10 MIN

SYD'S SLIDERS FOR A CROWD

Sliders are crowd-pleasers, and no one does them better than Syd. Rather than flipping the patties individually, he grills the burger in one big slab, then places it on a pack of halved Hawaiian rolls. Slice them up, right at the table, and serve with all the fixings—including my easy homemade pickles.

INGREDIENTS

QUICK PICKLES

½ English cucumber
4 lemons
½ cup water
1 teaspoon kosher salt
1 tablespoon granulated sugar

CHIPOTLE BURGER SAUCE

¼ cup mayonnaise
1 tablespoon sauce from a can of chipotles in adobo sauce
1 tablespoon ketchup
1 teaspoon red wine vinegar

BURGERS & ASSEMBLY

1 head green leaf lettuce
1 heirloom tomato
½ small white onion
1½ teaspoons kosher salt
1 teaspoon freshly cracked black pepper
¼ teaspoon cayenne pepper
½ teaspoon paprika
¾ teaspoon garlic powder
1 pound ground beef, 20% fat
1 (12-count) pack sweet Hawaiian rolls
2 tablespoons unsalted butter
1 tablespoon white sesame seeds
Neutral oil, such as avocado oil, for greasing the grill
8 slices cheddar

DIRECTIONS

Brine the Quick Pickles

1. Thinly slice the cucumber and set it aside in a 16-ounce jar. Juice the lemons and measure ½ cup juice. In a small saucepan combine the lemon juice, water, salt, and sugar. Bring to a boil and stir until the sugar and salt are completely dissolved. Pour the hot liquid over the sliced cucumbers, then cover and place in the fridge for at least 30 minutes and up to 4 days.

Prep the Burger Sauce & Veggies

2. Prepare the burger sauce by adding the mayonnaise, adobo sauce, ketchup, and red wine vinegar to a bowl. Whisk until smooth, then store in an airtight container in the fridge until ready to use.

3. Next, prepare the veggies. Wash and tear the lettuce, then thinly slice the tomato and onion and set aside.

Make the Burgers

4. Combine the salt, pepper, cayenne, paprika, and garlic powder in a small bowl. On a sheet of parchment paper, use your hands to press the ground beef into a rectangle approximately 10 x 7 ½ inches (about ½ inch larger than the package of Hawaiian rolls). Alternatively, layer another piece of parchment on top of the ground beef and roll it out with a rolling pin. Sprinkle the seasoning all over the top of the patty and let sit at room temperature for 10 to 15 minutes.

5. While the meat rests, preheat the grill to 250 degrees over low heat. Use a bread knife to slice the slab of Hawaiian rolls in half horizontally, like you're making a giant sandwich.

6. Melt the butter. Brush it across the tops of the buns and on both of the interior halves. Sprinkle the sesame seeds over the top of the buns. Place the buns on the grill, interior halves on the

Continued on next page →

grates, and cover. Cook for 2 to 3 minutes, checking on them frequently, until the buns are charred. Remove from the grill and set aside.

7. Turn the grill up to medium heat, preheating until it reaches 350 degrees. Grease the grates of the grill with a bit of oil. Using the parchment paper you shaped the meat on, transfer the patty to the grill, parchment side up. Immediately remove the parchment and cook the patty until the bottom is charred—about 3 minutes. Loosen the patty from the grill and flip, then immediately top with the sliced cheese and close the grill to melt for an additional 2 minutes.

8. Remove the patty from the grill and let rest for 5 minutes. Transfer the patty to the charred Hawaiian rolls, then replace the top bun and use a sharp knife to slice into individual sliders. Top each slider with burger sauce, pickles, lettuce, onion, and tomato as desired.

GRILLED SQUASH WITH WHIPPED FETA

Charring summer squash brings out its natural depth, while a grilled lemon's mellowed acidity adds a twist of brightness. The citrus is blended into feta, creating a smoky, smooth base. Finished with a sprinkle of fresh herbs and toasted almonds, this dish brings a refined touch to any barbeque spread.

INGREDIENTS

½ cup sliced almonds
Drizzle of extra-virgin olive oil
¼ teaspoon freshly cracked black pepper
1 pound zucchini
1 pound yellow squash
1 lemon
2 tablespoons extra-virgin olive oil, divided
¾ teaspoon kosher salt, divided
1 garlic clove
1 (7-ounce) block feta
⅔ cup fresh oregano leaves, divided
Red pepper flakes, for serving (optional)

TIP: Alternatively, serve the squash and whipped feta separately. You can also use the whipped feta as a dip for chips or other crudité vegetables.

DIRECTIONS

1. Add the sliced almonds and a drizzle of olive oil to a small skillet along with the pepper and a pinch of salt. Toast over medium heat for 3 to 4 minutes, or until fragrant and lightly golden. Set aside to cool.

2. Preheat the grill to 350 degrees over medium heat. Trim each end of the squash, then slice into spears—about 4 spears per zucchini and between 6 and 8 spears per yellow squash (depending on size). Slice the lemon in half crosswise. Toss the lemon halves and spears of squash with 1 tablespoon of the oil and ½ teaspoon of the salt.

3. Transfer the squash and lemon to the grill, placing everything cut side down. With the lid closed, grill for 5 minutes. Turn the squash and leave the lemon halves unturned, then cover and grill for an additional 5 minutes. At this point, the squash should be tender but al dente, bend slightly without breaking, and have dark grill marks on each side. The lemon halves will be intensely charred.

4. Set the grilled squash and one charred lemon half aside. Grate or mince the garlic into the bowl of a food processor. Break the feta into pieces and add it to the food processor along with ⅓ cup of the oregano leaves and the remaining ¼ teaspoon salt. Squeeze one of the charred lemon halves into the food processor and blend the feta on high speed. Gradually add the remaining 1 tablespoon oil and continue mixing until the feta is smooth and aerated—2 to 3 minutes.

5. To serve, spread the whipped feta on the bottom of a platter and top with the squash. Sprinkle the toasted almonds over the top, along with the remaining ⅓ cup of the oregano leaves, and add a few shakes of red pepper flakes (if using). Squeeze the remaining charred lemon over the top of the dish.

YIELD: 8 SERVINGS PREP: 25 MIN COOK: 15 MIN

CHARRED CORN SALAD WITH CILANTRO DRESSING

In the height of summer, all I want is a great salad filled with fresh produce. Featuring charred corn, peak summer tomatoes, and salty cotija, this is my go-to summer salad that checks all the boxes. I keep a jar of the cilantro dressing in our fridge, making it easy to have this salad anytime the craving strikes.

INGREDIENTS

CILANTRO DRESSING

½ jalapeño, seeds removed
1 garlic clove
1 cup cilantro leaves, loosely packed
⅓ cup sour cream
⅓ cup mayonnaise
¼ cup lime juice (about 2 limes)
1 teaspoon honey
½ teaspoon kosher salt

SALAD & ASSEMBLY

3 ears corn, shucked and trimmed
1 head romaine
1 heirloom tomato, about 1 pound
3 ounces Cotija, crumbled (about ⅔ cup)
½ cup roasted pepitas

DIRECTIONS

1. Roughly chop the jalapeño, garlic, and cilantro, then place them in a blender with the sour cream, mayonnaise, lime juice, honey, and salt. Blend until completely smooth, then store in an airtight container in the fridge until ready to use.

2. Preheat the grill to 400 degrees over medium-high heat and bring a large pot of heavily salted water to a boil on the stove. Parboil the corn for 5 minutes, then remove from the pot and transfer directly to the grill. Char the corn for 5 to 7 minutes, turning frequently to blister all sides. Remove the corn from the grill and allow it to cool slightly.

3. While the corn cools, chop the romaine and tomato and place in a large bowl.

4. Lay the corn on its side and slice the kernels from the cob. Add the corn, cotija, and roasted pepitas to the salad. Toss to combine.

5. Just before serving, toss the salad with the cilantro dressing to taste. Transfer to a large serving platter or bowl and enjoy.

NO RETORNABLE

YIELD: 12 SLICES | PREP: 20 MIN | COOK: 25 MIN | REST: 1 HR

GRANDMA GLO'S COLA CAKE

Childhood trips to my grandparents' home in North Carolina often fell on my birthday. Lucky for me, this meant "Happy Birthday" was sung over Grandma Glo's Cola Cake. It's a lush sheet cake with a dash of cinnamon and hint of cola, made only more satisfying with a scoop of ice cream.

INGREDIENTS

COLA CAKE

1 cup (226 grams) unsalted butter, plus more for greasing the pan
2 cups (260 grams) all-purpose flour, fluffed, scooped, and leveled
1¾ cups (347 grams) granulated sugar
¼ teaspoon ground cinnamon
1 teaspoon baking soda
1 teaspoon kosher salt
½ cup (114 grams) sour cream
2 eggs
1 tablespoon (14 grams) vanilla extract
1½ cups (341 grams) classic Coca-Cola
¼ cup (21 grams) unsweetened cocoa powder

COLA ICING

½ cup (113 grams) unsalted butter
2 tablespoons (10 grams) unsweetened cocoa powder
¼ teaspoon ground cinnamon
¼ teaspoon kosher salt
⅓ cup (76 grams) classic Coca-Cola
3¼ cups (390 grams) powdered sugar

DIRECTIONS

1. Preheat the oven to 350 degrees and grease an 18 x 13-inch sheet pan with butter. In a large bowl whisk together the flour, sugar, cinnamon, baking soda, and salt. In a separate medium bowl whisk together the sour cream, eggs, and vanilla until well combined.

2. Add the sour cream mixture to the flour mixture and mix with a rubber spatula until no dry spots remain. The batter should have a very thick, biscuit dough–like consistency.

3. Cut the butter into tablespoon-size pieces and melt it in a medium saucepan over medium heat. Add the cola and cocoa powder, then whisk to combine. Increase the heat to high and bring the mixture to a boil. Once boiling, whisk constantly for at least 1 minute and up to 2 minutes, until the mixture is smooth, bubbly, and barely thickened. Pour the hot cola mixture over the batter, then gently whisk until completely smooth and combined.

4. Pour the cake batter into the prepared sheet pan. Bake for 16 to 18 minutes, or until the cake is set and a toothpick inserted into the center emerges with a few moist crumbs.

5. After removing the cake from the oven, immediately make the icing. Melt the butter in a small saucepan over medium heat, then add the cocoa powder, cinnamon, and salt. Whisk to combine and remove from the heat. Add the cola and sift in the powdered sugar. Whisk until smooth.

6. Pour the icing over the warm cake and spread evenly with an offset spatula. Allow the cake to cool to room temperature, about 1 hour, and serve plain or with a scoop of Salted Vanilla Bean Ice Cream (pg. 159).

PHOTO: Grandma Glo on her farm in North Carolina.

YIELD: 8 DRINKS PREP: 20 MIN

WATERMELON RANCH WATER

Syd's love of Topo Chico runs deep. So deep that he has a dedicated fridge in his office. Although he's a Topo Chico purist, adding a splash of watermelon, shot of tequila (or not), and squeeze of lime turns it into a dewy summer cocktail. Don't skip salting the rim—it's a must to highlight the bubbles and tart citrus.

INGREDIENTS

2 pounds peeled and diced seedless watermelon
4 limes, plus more for serving
¼ teaspoon kosher salt, plus more for serving
2 (12-ounce) bottles Topo Chico mineral sparkling water, chilled
12 ounces tequila
1 jalapeño, thinly sliced (optional)
Ice, for serving

DIRECTIONS

1. Add the diced watermelon to a blender and blend on medium speed until juiced, 1 to 2 minutes. Strain the watermelon juice through a fine-mesh sieve to remove any pulp. Set aside in a pitcher or a large airtight container. You should have about 3 cups (24 ounces) of watermelon juice.

2. Juice the limes to yield about ½ cup. Add the lime juice and salt to the watermelon juice and stir to combine. Refrigerate until ready to drink.

3. To serve, salt the rim of a glass and add ice. Pour 3 ½ ounces watermelon juice into the glass, then top with 3 ounces Topo Chico, 1 ½ ounces tequila, and a few slices of jalapeños (if using). Garnish with an extra wedge of lime.

TIP: To make into a mocktail, use 3 ½ ounces of watermelon juice and 4 ounces of Topo Chico. Be sure to buy an extra 12-ounce bottle of Topo Chico to account for the extra mineral water.

CLASSIC SEAFOOD BOIL

ON THE MENU

CLASSIC SEAFOOD BOIL

GRILLED GARLIC BREAD

STRAWBERRIES & CREAM CAKE

ARNOLD PALMER

At the end of every summer, we roll up our sleeves and host a seafood boil in our backyard. One big pot, a simple setup, and the kind of lively energy that only comes from bounteous meals like this one. A classic red-and-white-checkered tablecloth is layered with brown craft paper that's both practical and part of the scene—ready to catch corn cobs, lemon wedges, and buttery crab shells as the evening unfolds. With the clatter of shells, hands reaching across the table for another helping, the warm breeze carrying the scent of butter and Old Bay through the air, this meal is as abundant as summer itself.

While I have perfected the right timing and a signature buttery herb sauce over the years, this menu maintains a classic seafood boil poured straight onto the table, as per tradition. I've added my grilled garlic bread for soaking up every drop of sauce, and a strawberries-and-cream cake that's as easygoing as it is impressive. An ice-cold pitcher of Arnold Palmers complements the day.

STYLING: *If you live in a buggy climate, incorporate citronella candles or fly fans as part of the decor.*

YIELD: 12 SERVINGS PREP: 45 MIN COOK: 45 MIN

CLASSIC SEAFOOD BOIL

Before we even moved in to our house, I pictured hosting our annual seafood boil in a backyard lined with hydrangeas. Most years we load the table with crab, shrimp, and lobster, but you can add more (or less) of whatever you like, so long as it has my signature herb butter to tie it all together.

INGREDIENTS

SEAFOOD BOIL

2 yellow onions
1 garlic bulb
2 lemons
6 ears corn, shucked and trimmed
1½ pounds andouille sausage
½ cup unsalted butter
12 quarts water
1½ cups Old Bay seasoning
5 dried bay leaves
½ cup kosher salt
2 pounds baby potatoes, such as red or Yukon Gold
1½ pounds uncooked littleneck clams, scrubbed
2½ pounds uncooked snow crab or lobster tails
2 pounds uncooked jumbo shrimp, peeled and deveined

SIGNATURE HERB BUTTER

½ cup fresh flat-leaf parsley, packed
1 bunch fresh chives, about 1 cup minced
3 lemons, divided
5 garlic cloves
1 cup unsalted butter
1 tablespoon Old Bay seasoning
1 teaspoon kosher salt
¼ cup boiling liquid from the seafood boil

DIRECTIONS

1. Quarter the onions, halve the garlic bulb horizontally, and slice the lemons. Cut each ear of corn into thirds, then slice the andouille into 2-inch pieces. Set everything aside separately.

2. In a 20-quart stockpot, melt the butter over medium-low heat. Add the onion and garlic and cook, stirring frequently, for 4 to 5 minutes.

3. Next, add the water, sliced lemons, Old Bay seasoning, bay leaves, and salt to the pot and bring to a boil. Boil, uncovered, for 10 minutes. Add the baby potatoes, then boil for an additional 10 minutes. Add the corn and boil for 5 minutes.

4. Transfer the andouille, clams, and crab or lobster to the pot, submerging the seafood under the water. Boil for 5 minutes, then add the shrimp. Boil for 3 to 4 minutes, or until the crab or lobster is vibrant orange, and the shrimp is pink but not yet curled.

5. Remove from heat and reserve ¼ cup of the boiling liquid. Strain the rest of the liquid, then cover the seafood, sausage, and veggies with aluminum foil.

6. Finally, prepare the butter. Finely chop the parsley and chives, zest 1 lemon, and mince the garlic. To a small saucepan add the parsley, chives, 1 tablespoon of the lemon zest, garlic, butter, Old Bay, and salt. Place the butter mixture over medium heat and cook until it is completely melted, 4 to 5 minutes. Add the reserved boiling liquid and whisk to combine.

7. Serve the seafood boil on a platter or pour it directly onto the table. Drizzle about half of the butter over the top, then place the rest in bowls along the table. Cut the remaining 2 lemons into wedges and serve with the seafood boil.

YIELD: 12 SERVINGS PREP: 10 MIN COOK: 7 MIN

GRILLED GARLIC BREAD

With five ingredients and about fifteen minutes, you can throw together a garlic bread that's not to be overlooked. It's loaded with garlic and cheese, then quickly charred on the grill. The bread comes off the flame smoky and crisp—a great side for mopping up extra butter from the Classic Seafood Boil (pg. 131).

INGREDIENTS

4 tablespoons extra-virgin olive oil, plus more for the grill
1 loaf French bread
½ teaspoon kosher salt
6 garlic cloves
½ cup finely grated Parmigiano-Reggiano

DIRECTIONS

1. Clean your grill grates and brush lightly with oil before starting the grill. Preheat the grill over medium-low heat until the temperature reaches about 250 degrees.

2. While the grill preheats, slice the French bread in half horizontally, as if preparing to make a sandwich.

3. Add the oil and salt to a small bowl. Grate the garlic into the oil, add the Parmigiano-Reggiano, and whisk to combine. Spread the oil mixture generously over each half of bread.

4. Place the bread on the grill, spread-side up, and cook with the lid open for 2 to 3 minutes. Flip the bread face down, so the spread is in contact with the grates. Grill for an additional 3 to 4 minutes with the lid open, checking the bread frequently, until the bread features dark grill marks.

5. Remove the bread from the grill and slice into smaller pieces before serving.

YIELD: 12 SLICES | PREP: 30 MIN | COOK: 40 MIN | REST: 2 HR 30 MIN

STRAWBERRIES & CREAM CAKE

Every year our county holds a weeklong rodeo called Strawberry Days. While we love the festivities, the real highlight is the fresh strawberries bathed in sweetened cream. This cake captures that same indulgence, and the heaping pile of strawberries is a nod to carefree summer days.

INGREDIENTS

BUTTERMILK CAKE

Unsalted butter, for greasing the pan
3 cups (390 grams) cake flour, fluffed, scooped, and leveled
2 teaspoons baking powder
¼ teaspoon baking soda
1 teaspoon kosher salt
1 cup (198 grams) neutral oil, such as avocado oil
1 cup (198 grams) granulated sugar
½ cup (156 grams) sweetened condensed milk
3 eggs, room temperature
1 tablespoon vanilla bean paste or vanilla extract
1¼ cup (284 grams) buttermilk, room temperature

SWEETENED WHIPPED CREAM & ASSEMBLY

1 pound strawberries
1 cup (227 grams) heavy whipping cream, cold
½ cup (156 grams) sweetened condensed milk
½ teaspoon kosher salt

TIP: Nothing about this cake is too precious; in fact, the more rustic, the better.

DIRECTIONS

1. Preheat the oven to 350 degrees and lightly grease two 8-inch cake pans with butter. In a large bowl whisk together the cake flour, baking powder, baking soda, and salt. Set aside.

2. Add the oil and sugar to the bowl of a stand mixer fitted with a paddle attachment and beat on medium speed until lightly creamed, 2 to 3 minutes. Add the sweetened condensed milk and mix for 1 minute. The mixture will look curdled.

3. Add the eggs and vanilla to the milk mixture. Whisk on medium speed for 30 seconds to 1 minute until the mixture is smooth and combined. Next add the flour mixture in two parts, mixing on low for about 60 seconds between additions. Pour in the buttermilk, then mix until just combined.

4. Transfer the batter to the prepared pans. Bake for 35 to 38 minutes, or until the cake springs back under a gentle press of the finger or a toothpick comes out with a few moist, spongy crumbs. Let the cakes cool for 30 minutes, then turn them out onto a cooling rack to rest for another 2 hours.

5. While the cake cools, hull and dice half of the strawberries, then hull and slice the other half and set aside. In the bowl of a stand mixer fitted with a whisk attachment, combine the cream, sweetened condensed milk, and salt. Whisk on medium-high speed for 2 to 3 minutes, or until the whipped cream is thick and fluffy with medium peaks.

6. To assemble the cake, use a serrated knife to level one of the cake rounds. Add it to a cake stand or plate, then top with about half of the diced strawberries and half of the whipped cream. Set the second cake round on top, dome-side up. Gently press down, then pile the remaining whipped cream on top of the cake, using the back of a spoon to create swoops and swirls in the cream. Pile the sliced strawberries on top. Chill until ready to serve.

YIELD: 12 DRINKS | PREP: 15 MIN | COOK: 5 MIN | REST: 6 HRS

ARNOLD PALMER

Setting out a shared pitcher of Arnold Palmers makes hosting easy—just place it next to a stack of glasses and let your guests serve themselves. Part tea, part lemonade, this drink is homespun, unfussy, and it evokes memories of summer days spent on a porch swing.

INGREDIENTS

7 cups water, divided
1½ cups granulated sugar
3 black tea or rooibos tea bags
11 to 13 lemons
¼ teaspoon kosher salt
18 ounces vodka (optional)

DIRECTIONS

1. In a small saucepan make a simple syrup by combining 1 ½ cups of the water with the sugar over high heat. Bring the mixture to a boil, whisking frequently. Continue boiling for 3 to 4 minutes until the sugar is completely dissolved.

2. Remove the simple syrup from the heat and add the tea bags to the hot syrup. Let steep for 7 to 8 minutes, then remove the tea bags and pour the syrup into a large pitcher.

3. Juice the lemons and measure 2 cups of juice. Add the lemon juice, salt, and the remaining 5 ½ cups water to the pitcher. Stir to combine and chill for at least 6 hours or overnight.

4. To serve, add 6 ounces of the Arnold Palmer to a glass and top with 1 ½ ounces vodka. Alternatively, add all of the vodka directly to the batch of Arnold Palmer, stir to combine, and serve right from the pitcher.

TIP: To make this drink a mocktail, simply leave out the vodka and drink as is. Add 1 to 2 additional cups of water if desired.

PIZZA NIGHT

ON THE MENU

PERFECT PIZZA DOUGH

GO-TO TOMATO SAUCE

FONTINA APPLE PIZZA

HOT HONEY PIZZA

GREEN GODDESS PIZZA

SAUSAGE & MUSHROOM PIZZA

PEACH BURRATA SALAD

S'MORES COOKIE SKILLET

SALTED VANILLA BEAN ICE CREAM

Our favorite summer evenings are the ones spent under the café lights, with pizzas flying in and out of the oven and friends gathered around a folding table, lingering late into the night. Syd has a serious love for pizza—he once set a personal record visiting seven different pizza spots in one day in New York City—and over the years, it's become a passion we share. We love pizza with homemade sauce, a crust that's supple yet well-fired, and a blend of classic and unexpected combinations. Hosting pizza night has become one of our favorite ways to hang out. It's a simple setup, with ingredients prepped ahead and an open invitation for everyone to build, bake, and enjoy.

With the apple trees overhead and the glow of lights strung through the branches, the menu is casual but crafted with care. The pizzas are a mix of hearty essentials like sausage and mushroom and bright flavors like fontina and apple, all paired with a peach burrata salad that practically tastes like summer. Last to the table is a gooey s'mores cookie skillet served warm with homemade salted vanilla bean ice cream. It's a night made for second slices, barefoot kids running through the grass, and conversation that stretches long after the last pizza leaves the oven.

STYLING: *Tiny potted plants in groupings down the table make excellent centerpieces that bring an organic touch to both casual and formal settings.*

YIELD: 4 10-OUNCE BALLS PREP: 35 MIN REST: 5 HR 20 MIN

PERFECT PIZZA DOUGH

We are pizza people through and through, whether it's a New York pizza crawl or pies made at home. Our ideal crust is soft yet sturdy, with a good char on the edges. This recipe meets all the requirements. Best of all, the rising time is quite flexible, so you can have pizza on the table anytime you want.

INGREDIENTS

5 cups (650 grams) 00 flour
1 teaspoon fast-rising instant yeast
1 tablespoon (10 grams) kosher salt
1 tablespoon (13 grams) extra-virgin olive oil
2 cups (454 grams) water

DIRECTIONS

1. Add the flour, yeast, salt, and oil to a large bowl. Warm the water to 110 degrees, then add to the bowl. Using your hands, mix the ingredients into a sticky, shaggy dough. Cover the bowl with a towel and let rest for 20 minutes.

2. Transfer the dough to a lightly floured work surface. Working quickly to prevent sticking, knead the dough for 3 to 4 minutes or until it is smooth and elastic. This dough is tacky but should be workable. Lightly re-flour the work surface, only as needed, to prevent excess sticking.

3. Divide the dough into fourths (about 270 grams each). Form each portion into a ball by cupping your hand against the side of the dough and dragging it across the counter a few times.

4. Place the dough in lightly oiled airtight containers. Proof for 4 to 5 hours at room temperature, or 8 to 18 hours in the fridge. The dough is done proofing when it has doubled in size. If refrigerating, let the dough rest at room temperature for 1 hour before using.

TO MAKE THE PIZZAS WITHOUT A PIZZA OVEN

1. Stretch the dough into a 10-inch round. Place a rack in the top third of the oven and turn on the broiler. On the stovetop, preheat a 12-inch cast-iron skillet over medium-high heat until a sprinkle of water evaporates instantly.

2. Place the dough (no toppings) in the skillet and cook for 3 to 4 minutes. Spin and check the bottom of the crust occasionally until it is charred with leopard-like spots.

3. Off the heat, add the toppings. Place the skillet under the broiler for 2 to 3 minutes, watching closely, until the crust is browned and the cheese is melted and bubbly. Top the pizza with any fresh ingredients, slice, and serve.

BIA
DiNAP
Whole Peeled Tomatoes
NET WT 28 OZ (1 LB 12 OZ)

YIELD: 3 CUPS PREP: 5 MIN COOK: 30 MIN

GO-TO TOMATO SAUCE

Once I started making my own tomato sauce, I swore off anything jarred. It's as simple as it gets—just four basic ingredients and thirty minutes on the stove. I always prepare the sauce a day or two ahead of time so that pizza night is a breeze. Aside from being convenient, the sauce gets even better as it sits.

INGREDIENTS

1 (28-ounce) can whole peeled tomatoes
1 garlic clove
1 sprig fresh basil
2 teaspoons kosher salt

DIRECTIONS

1. Add the tomatoes to a saucepan, crushing the whole tomatoes in your hands as you transfer them. Grate the garlic into the tomatoes, then add the basil sprig and salt. Stir to combine.

2. Bring the sauce to a simmer over medium-low heat. Reduce the heat to low and simmer for 30 minutes, uncovered, stirring occasionally. Remove the basil sprig and allow the sauce to cool to room temperature before assembling pizza. If preparing ahead, store in an airtight container in the fridge for 5 to 6 days.

YIELD: 1 12-INCH PIZZA PREP: 15 MIN COOK: 2 MIN

FONTINA APPLE PIZZA

During a trip to southern France, Syd and I had a fontina apple pizza that we are still thinking about, even today. After several tests, we created this version that has been in our regular rotation ever since. The apples stay firm, the cheese is melty, and it transports us right back to coastal France.

INGREDIENTS

¼ small Honeycrisp apple, skin on
¼ small shallot
1 (10-ounce) ball Perfect Pizza Dough (pg. 143)
2 tablespoons heavy whipping cream
1 cup grated fontina
½ bunch watercress

DIRECTIONS

1. Preheat the pizza oven to between 725 and 750 degrees. Thinly slice the apples and shallot.

2. On a lightly floured work surface or pizza peel, stretch the dough into a 12-inch round, starting at the center and working outward. Lift the dough by the edge and quickly rotate it as gravity pulls it toward the counter. Place the dough on the pizza peel and gently shake back and forth to ensure that it doesn't stick.

3. Top the pizza with the cream, then add the fontina cheese, apple slices, and shallot slices.

4. Using the pizza peel, launch the pizza into the pizza oven. Cook the pizza for about 90 seconds, turning it every 10 to 15 seconds, until the cheese is melted and the crust is charred with leopard-like spots around the edges.

5. Transfer the pizza to a wire rack to cool—this helps create a crisper crust. Top with a small handful of watercress, then slice and enjoy.

TIP: To make this pizza without a pizza oven, see instructions on pg. 143.

YIELD: 1 12-INCH PIZZA PREP: 15 MIN COOK: 10 MIN

HOT HONEY PIZZA

Inspired by a local pizza spot, Mozz, this is Syd's favorite pie in our lineup. The pizza is layered with fresh mozzarella and your choice of speck, prosciutto, or pepperoni, but the real showstopper is a drizzle of homemade honey. It's spicy yet sweet, with a flavor that store-bought just can't replicate.

INGREDIENTS

SERRANO HOT HONEY

1 serrano chili
½ cup honey
½ teaspoon lemon juice or apple cider vinegar

PIZZA & ASSEMBLY

1 (10-ounce) ball Perfect Pizza Dough (pg. 143)
¼ cup Go-To Tomato Sauce (pg. 145)
3½ ounces fresh mozzarella
2 tablespoons whole-milk ricotta
1 ounce speck, prosciutto, or pepperoni

TIPS: Make the hot honey a day ahead, just to keep things easy.

To make this pizza without a pizza oven, see instructions on pg. 143.

DIRECTIONS

1. Preheat the pizza oven to between 725 and 750 degrees. To make the hot honey, thinly slice the serrano and add it to a small saucepan with the honey. Warm over medium heat until the honey just begins to foam and sizzle, 5 to 7 minutes, then remove from the heat. Add the lemon juice or vinegar and whisk to combine. Set aside to cool.

2. On a lightly floured work surface or pizza peel, stretch the dough into a 12-inch round, starting at the center and working outward. Lift the dough by the edge and quickly rotate it as gravity pulls it toward the counter. Place the dough on a pizza peel and gently shake back and forth to ensure that it doesn't stick.

3. Top the pizza with the tomato sauce and tear the fresh mozzarella onto the pizza. Dollop with ricotta, then tear the speck or prosciutto over the pizza or top with pepperoni.

4. Using the pizza peel, launch the pizza into the pizza oven. Cook the pizza for about 90 seconds, turning it every 10 to 15 seconds, until the cheese is melted and the crust is charred with leopard-like spots around the edges.

5. Transfer the pizza to a wire rack to cool—this helps create a crisper crust. Drizzle with the hot honey, slice, and enjoy.

YIELD: 1 12-INCH PIZZA PREP: 20 MIN COOK: 2 MIN

GREEN GODDESS PIZZA

It took many iterations to get this green goddess dressing just right, and it was worth every attempt. This herb-packed dressing is slathered onto the pizza, dotted with goat cheese, then topped with spring greens piled high on the crust.

INGREDIENTS

GREEN GODDESS DRESSING

2 lemons
½ cup marinated artichoke hearts, drained
2 tablespoons roughly chopped fresh chives
1 tablespoon roughly chopped fresh tarragon
2 tablespoons roughly chopped fresh flat-leaf parsley
1 garlic clove
¾ teaspoon granulated sugar
¼ teaspoon kosher salt
¼ teaspoon freshly cracked black pepper
½ cup heavy whipping cream

PIZZA & ASSEMBLY

1 (10-ounce) ball Perfect Pizza Dough (pg. 143)
2 ounces goat cheese
½ small watermelon radish (optional)
2 ounces spring mix
1 tablespoon toasted pine nuts, for serving

DIRECTIONS

1. Preheat the pizza oven to between 725 and 750 degrees. Juice the lemons and measure ¼ cup juice. Make the green goddess dressing by adding the lemon juice, artichokes, chives, tarragon, parsley, garlic, sugar, salt, and pepper to a blender. Blend until smooth, then add the cream and pulse for another 15 to 20 seconds until combined. Store in an airtight container in the fridge until ready to use.

2. On a lightly floured work surface or pizza peel, stretch the dough into a 12-inch round, starting at the center and working outward. Lift the dough by the edge and quickly rotate it as gravity pulls it toward the counter. Place the dough on a pizza peel and gently shake back and forth to ensure that it doesn't stick.

3. Top the pizza with 3 tablespoons green goddess dressing and dot with goat cheese.

4. Using the pizza peel, launch the pizza into the pizza oven. Cook the pizza for about 90 seconds, turning it every 10 to 15 seconds, until the goat cheese begins to brown and the crust is charred with leopard-like spots around the edges.

5. Transfer the pizza to a wire rack to cool—this helps create a crisper crust. If using, thinly slice the watermelon radish and add it to a bowl with the spring mix. Toss the salad with more green goddess dressing, to taste, and pile it onto the pizza. Top with the pine nuts, then slice and enjoy.

TIP: To make this pizza without a pizza oven, see instructions on pg. 143.

YIELD: 1 12-INCH PIZZA PREP: 10 MIN COOK: 20 MIN

SAUSAGE & MUSHROOM PIZZA

This is a hearty pizza, topped with ample mushrooms and sausage. Perhaps best of all, it's loaded with mozzarella to give the pizza an intensely melty cheese pull. The key to amazing flavor is letting the mushrooms sit in your skillet, undisturbed, to caramelize and develop a pronounced umami flavor.

INGREDIENTS

4 ounces mixed mushrooms, such as cremini, oyster, shiitake, and/or trumpet
1 teaspoon extra-virgin olive oil
¼ pound ground Italian sausage
1 (10-ounce) ball Perfect Pizza Dough (pg. 143)
¼ cup Go-To Tomato Sauce (pg. 145)
1 cup grated mozzarella, packed

DIRECTIONS

1. Preheat the pizza oven to between 725 and 750 degrees. Tear the mushrooms into irregular pieces and set aside. Warm the oil in a skillet over medium-high heat, then add the sausage and cook for 8 to 10 minutes, or until cooked through and slightly caramelized. Using a slotted spoon, remove the sausage from the skillet and reduce the heat to medium low.

2. Place the torn mushrooms in the skillet and leave them undisturbed for 3 to 4 minutes. Turn the mushrooms, then let them cook (again undisturbed) for an additional 3 to 4 minutes. Once golden brown, remove the mushrooms from the skillet.

3. On a lightly floured work surface or pizza peel, stretch the dough into a 12-inch round, starting at the center and working outward. Lift the dough by the edge and quickly rotate it as gravity pulls it toward the counter. Place the dough on a pizza peel and gently shake back and forth to ensure that it doesn't stick.

4. Top the pizza with the tomato sauce and mozzarella, then top with the crumbled sausage and mushrooms.

5. Using the pizza peel, launch the pizza into the pizza oven. Cook the pizza for about 90 seconds, turning it every 10 to 15 seconds, until the cheese is melted and the crust is charred with leopard-like spots around the edges.

6. Transfer the pizza to a wire rack to cool—this helps create a crisper crust. Slice and enjoy.

TIP: To make this pizza without a pizza oven, see instructions on pg. 143.

YIELD: 6 SERVINGS | PREP: 20 MIN | COOK: 7 MIN

PEACH BURRATA SALAD

To me, cooking feels like a design project as much as it does an approach to flavor. This salad is all about juxtaposition—juicy peaches, peppery arugula, and milky burrata create a flavor and color story as summery as the season itself. It's one of my favorite seasonal salads, and it pairs with just about anything.

INGREDIENTS

HONEY BALSAMIC VINAIGRETTE

¼ cup extra-virgin olive oil
3 tablespoons balsamic vinegar
2 tablespoons honey
½ teaspoon kosher salt
½ teaspoon freshly cracked black pepper

SALAD & ASSEMBLY

1 cup walnut halves
1½ teaspoons extra-virgin olive oil
1½ teaspoons honey
½ teaspoon kosher salt
½ teaspoon red pepper flakes (optional)
5 ounces arugula
1 pound fresh peaches
8 ounces burrata

DIRECTIONS

1. Prepare the vinaigrette by adding the oil, vinegar, honey, salt, and pepper to a large bowl. Whisk vigorously until the vinaigrette is completely blended with a thick, glossy viscosity. Set aside.

2. In a small bowl toss the walnut halves with the oil, honey, salt, and red pepper flakes (if using). Heat a skillet over medium heat, add the walnuts, and toast the nuts for 5 to 7 minutes or until fragrant and golden. Remove from heat and allow to cool.

3. Toss the arugula in the vinaigrette, then pile it on a large serving platter. There should still be vinaigrette in the bottom of the bowl. Slice the peaches into eighths and add to the bowl with the remaining vinaigrette. Toss the peaches to coat them in the vinaigrette.

4. Spoon the peaches over the top of the dressed arugula, drizzling any extra dressing over the top of the greens. Tear the burrata into pieces and arrange around the salad, then roughly chop the walnuts and sprinkle over the top. Serve and enjoy immediately.

YIELD: 6–8 SERVINGS PREP: 25 MIN COOK: 18 MIN

S'MORES COOKIE SKILLET

Many of our summer nights are spent making s'mores. Syd is on fire duty, and the girls and I manage gooey marshmallows, unevenly snapped graham crackers, and chocolate bars. Inspired by those evenings, enjoy this shareable skillet tableside with a big scoop of Salted Vanilla Bean Ice Cream (pg. 159).

INGREDIENTS

- 12 rectangular graham cracker sheets (186 grams), divided
- 1 cup (130 grams) all-purpose flour, fluffed, scooped, and leveled
- ¾ teaspoon baking soda
- 1 teaspoon kosher salt
- ½ cup (113 grams) unsalted butter, softened
- ½ cup (107 grams) firmly packed light brown sugar
- ½ cup (99 grams) granulated sugar
- 1 egg
- 2 teaspoons vanilla extract
- 1 cup (60 grams) mini marshmallows, packed
- 10 large marshmallows (60 grams)
- ½ cup (85 grams) chopped 72% dark chocolate
- 1 king-size (73 grams) Hershey's milk chocolate bar, chopped, plus more for serving

TIP: If you have leftovers, warm them in the microwave for a few seconds to transform the cookie back into a warm, gooey treat.

DIRECTIONS

1. Preheat the oven to 375 degrees, then lightly butter a 12-inch cast-iron skillet and set aside.

2. Add 9 of the graham cracker sheets to the bowl of a food processor. Process until the graham crackers become a fine powder, 1 to 2 minutes. Combine the graham cracker crumbs with the flour, baking soda, and salt and sct asidc.

3. In the bowl of a stand mixer, beat the butter, brown sugar, and granulated sugar on medium speed until creamed, 3 to 4 minutes. Scrape the sides of the bowl, then add the egg and vanilla. Mix again for 1 to 2 minutes or until emulsified, smooth, and airy.

4. Add the graham cracker mixture to the stand mixer and beat on medium-high speed to combine, scraping the sides of the bowl halfway through. This should take no longer than 1 minute.

5. Add the mini marshmallows, the large marshmallows, the dark chocolate, and the Hershey's milk chocolate to the cookie dough. Break the remaining 3 graham cracker sheets into the dough. The pieces can stay fairly large. Beat once more to combine, about 1 minute. During this time, the graham cracker pieces will break and some of the large marshmallows will tear.

6. Press the cookie dough into the prepared skillet and transfer to the oven. Bake for 16 to 18 minutes, or until the sides are set and golden and the center is a bit underdone. If desired, press a few more squares of Hershey's chocolate into the top of the warm cookie. Let cool slightly, then serve with ice cream and enjoy immediately.

YIELD: 1 QUART PREP: 35 MIN REST: 18 HR

SALTED VANILLA BEAN ICE CREAM

I could speak in love notes about this ice cream. It's excellent with the s'mores cookie skillet, but there isn't a single dessert in this cookbook (or the world) that wouldn't be made better with a scoop. It's creamy, sweet, and pleasantly salty with flecks of vanilla bean throughout. Honestly, what's not to love?

INGREDIENTS

- 1 vanilla bean pod
- 2 ½ cups (568 grams) heavy whipping cream
- ¾ cup (170 grams) whole milk
- 2 teaspoons vanilla bean paste
- ¾ cup (149 grams) granulated sugar
- ¼ teaspoon xanthan gum
- ½ teaspoon kosher salt
- 1 teaspoon flaky salt

DIRECTIONS

1. Before you begin, make sure your ice cream maker is ready to go. Many models require freezing the bowl ahead of time (usually overnight).

2. Place a dry skillet over high heat until extremely hot. Add the vanilla bean pod and turn frequently until the sides are charred and the pod has puffed, 30 to 45 seconds. Remove the pod from the pan and let cool slightly to deflate. This makes it easier to remove the vanilla seeds and intensifies the vanilla flavor.

3. While the vanilla bean cools, in a large bowl whisk together the cream, milk, and vanilla bean paste to create the ice cream base. Slit the vanilla bean pod down the center lengthwise, then use the back of the knife to scrape the vanilla seeds from the pod. Add the seeds to the cream mixture and whisk to combine. Discard the pod or reserve for another use.

4. In a separate bowl whisk together the sugar, xanthan gum, and kosher salt. Add the sugar mixture to the ice cream base and whisk thoroughly to combine. Store in an airtight container in the fridge for 12 hours.

5. Pour the ice cream base into your ice cream machine and churn for 20 minutes, or according to your ice cream maker's instructions. About 2 minutes before the ice cream finishes churning, slowly sprinkle in the flaky salt. Quickly transfer the ice cream to a freezer-friendly container and freeze in the coldest part of your freezer until firm, at least 6 hours.

TIP: If you can't find vanilla bean paste, you can substitute vanilla extract in a one-to-one exchange.

BEACH PICNIC

ON THE MENU

TURKEY BEACH SANDWICH WITH KALE CASHEW PESTO

BLACKBERRY GOUDA SKEWERS

PICNIC POTATO CHIPS

McGEE'S ULTIMATE BROWNIE

There's a part of me that will always feel at home when I'm near the ocean. Syd grew up in Southern California, and we spent the first six years of our marriage there, with countless days spent tucked into the sand, salty and sun-warmed. Those early memories shaped what a perfect beach day looks like to me: a cozy blanket, a well-packed picnic, and the steady lull of waves setting the tone of the backdrop.

This menu is made for that kind of day. It includes sturdy sandwiches layered with turkey and kale pesto, crisp potato chips that somehow taste even better by the water, and a little something sweet tucked in for good measure. It's food that holds up in an icy cooler and is made to be eaten by hand, with sea mist on your skin and the horizon stretched wide in front of you.

STYLING: *All you need is one beautiful blanket and to let the view do the talking. As the host, focus on the functionality of preparing for the elements with a reliable cooler and airtight containers.*

Issue 38
Interiors, Art, Architecture, Travel, Style
Asia Pacific Edition
luxuryportfolio.com

YIELD: 6 SANDWICHES PREP: 30 MIN

TURKEY BEACH SANDWICH WITH KALE CASHEW PESTO

This isn't your everyday turkey sandwich. What really sets it apart is the kale cashew pesto, which is as nutrient dense as it is dynamic. Slather it on a great sandwich (like this one), toss it with pasta, or dollop it on salmon. The options are endless.

INGREDIENTS

KALE CASHEW PESTO

1 cup raw cashews
3 cups chopped curly-leaf kale, stems removed
1 cup fresh basil leaves, loosely packed
1 garlic clove
½ teaspoon kosher salt
½ cup extra-virgin olive oil

SANDWICH ASSEMBLY

6 ciabatta rolls
1¼ pounds smoked turkey, sandwich sliced
½ pound (about 12 slices) Havarti
1 (16-ounce) jar roasted red peppers, drained
¼ red onion
4 ounces arugula
4 ounces alfalfa sprouts
Balsamic vinegar and kosher salt, to taste

DIRECTIONS

1. Make the kale cashew pesto by adding the cashews, kale, basil, garlic, and salt to a food processor. Pulse until the mixture is roughly chopped. While processing on low speed, slowly pour the olive oil into the pesto and blend until combined. Make up to 5 days ahead of time and refrigerate until ready to use.

2. To assemble the sandwiches, slice each ciabatta roll in half horizontally and scoop out a bit of the middle to make the sandwich easier to assemble. Divide the turkey between each sandwich, draping it in irregular shapes on the bottom slice of the bread. Top the turkey with cheese, using about two slices per sandwich, and lay the peppers on top of the cheese.

3. Thinly slice the onion, then divide between each sandwich. Pile with arugula and alfalfa sprouts.

4. Sparingly drizzle balsamic vinegar over the top of the arugula and season with salt.

5. Spread the pesto on the top slices of ciabatta, using about 2 tablespoons per sandwich. Sandwich the bread together and press down gently. Wrap in parchment, if desired, and slice in half right before serving.

YIELD: 30–32 SKEWERS PREP: 40 MIN

BLACKBERRY GOUDA SKEWERS

Color and texture are top of mind when creating a menu. These skewers have a contrast of dark and light hues with a pleasant toasty crunch from coarse salt and walnuts. They're essentially a portable salad, easy to eat and transport whether I'm at the beach, hosting a barbeque, or sneaking a few into lunchboxes.

INGREDIENTS

1 pound peeled, deseeded honeydew melon
5 ounces Gouda
32 (4 ¾-inch) bamboo skewers
5 ounces spring mix
1 pint blackberries
½ cup walnut halves
Balsamic glaze, for serving
Coarse gray French salt, for serving

DIRECTIONS

1. Chop the honeydew into 1-inch cubes. Next, dice the Gouda into ½-inch cubes.

2. Assemble by layering a piece of honeydew, pinch of spring mix, cube of Gouda, blackberry, another pinch of spring mix, and another piece of honeydew on a skewer. Place in an airtight container or cover with plastic wrap, then refrigerate until ready to serve.

3. Meanwhile, toast the walnuts in a small nonstick skillet over medium heat for 5 to 7 minutes until fragrant. Finely chop.

4. To serve, set the skewers on a platter and drizzle with balsamic glaze, then sprinkle with the toasted walnuts and French salt. Alternatively, let guests dress the skewers on their own.

TRAVEL
LIFESTYLE
Interiors, Art, Architecture, Travel, Style
VOLUME 14 / ISSUE NO. 2
Issue 38

YIELD: 6 SERVINGS PREP: 30 MIN REST: 1 HR 30 MIN COOK: 30 MIN

PICNIC POTATO CHIPS

As soon as these homemade potato chips come out of the oil, you can find every one of us hovered over the cooling rack, ready to grab a handful. This recipe is foolproof, and the seasoning blend hits every tastebud.

INGREDIENTS

2½ pounds russet potatoes
3 pints peanut oil

SEASONING BLEND

4 tablespoons nutritional yeast
1½ teaspoons kosher salt
½ teaspoon onion powder
½ teaspoon granulated sugar
½ teaspoon freshly cracked black pepper

DIRECTIONS

1. Using a mandoline, thinly slice the potatoes to approximately 0.75 mm thick—not paper thin, but still thin enough to see light through the center.

2. Place the sliced potatoes in a bowl of cold water and let rest for 1 hour, switching the water halfway through and occasionally massaging the potatoes.

3. Drain the potato slices. Dry them with a salad spinner, then lay them in a single layer on clean towels to finish drying (a very small amount of residual moisture is okay), about 30 minutes.

4. While the potatoes dry, prepare the seasoning blend by combining the nutritional yeast, salt, onion powder, sugar, and pepper in a blender or food processor. Pulse until the spices are a fine powder, then set aside.

5. Place a cooling rack over an 18 x 13-inch sheet pan and line the rack with paper towels. Set it next to the stove. Add the peanut oil to a large, heavy-bottomed Dutch oven and place over medium heat.

6. Once the oil reaches 350 degrees or sizzles vigorously when you add a potato, work in about four batches and gently add the sliced potatoes. Fry for 5 to 7 minutes, or until the potatoes curl and turn an amber, golden brown. As they fry, stir frequently with a strainer or skimmer.

7. Transfer the potato chips to the prepared rack. Working quickly, sprinkle the seasoning over the hot chips. Store the chips in a paper bag for up to one week.

YIELD: 9 BROWNIES PREP: 45 MIN COOK: 1 HR

McGEE'S ULTIMATE BROWNIE

A few years ago, I had a life-changing brownie at Borough Market. I came home and began testing, determined to create a brownie just as fudgy and dense as the one I had in London. The key ingredient is self-rising flour. Don't try making your own—grab a bag from the store and start baking.

INGREDIENTS

- 1 cup (226 grams) unsalted butter, plus more for greasing the pan
- 1 cup (170 grams) milk chocolate chips
- 1 cup (170 grams) chopped 72% dark chocolate, or chips
- ½ cup (42 grams) Dutch-process cocoa powder
- ½ teaspoon kosher salt
- 2 cups (396 grams) granulated sugar
- 3 eggs
- 2 cups (260 grams) self-rising flour, fluffed, scooped, and leveled
- 1½ cups (255 grams) semisweet chocolate chips

TIP: To slice perfect brownie squares, slice the brownie in thirds, then turn the brownies 180 degrees and repeat.

DIRECTIONS

1. Preheat the oven to 325 degrees. Lightly grease a 9 x 9-inch pan with butter and line with parchment paper, trimming it to fit the width of the pan while leaving a few inches of parchment hanging over the edges of the two opposing sides.

2. In a small saucepan melt the butter, milk chocolate chips, and dark chocolate over medium-low heat until smooth. Remove from heat, then add the cocoa powder and salt and whisk to combine. Allow the mixture to cool for 10 to 15 minutes, or until it is still warm but no longer hot (about 125 degrees).

3. Meanwhile, add the sugar and eggs to the bowl of a stand mixer fitted with a whisk attachment. Whisk on medium-high speed for 5 minutes until the sugar mostly dissolves into the eggs and the texture is aerated with a very light, butter yellow color. You may still see sugar granules.

4. Add the cooled chocolate mixture to the eggs and whisk on medium speed until combined, scraping the sides of the bowl as needed. Remove the bowl from the stand mixer and use a spatula to fold the self-rising flour into the wet ingredients. When nearly combined, add the semisweet chocolate chips and finish mixing until the batter is smooth.

5. Transfer the brownie batter to the prepared pan. Bake, undisturbed, for 50 to 60 minutes or until the sides are set and the center still jiggles slightly. When inserted into the center, a toothpick should come out a bit gooey with several fudgy crumbs.

6. Remove the brownies from the oven and allow them to cool to room temperature. Once completely cooled, use the overhanging parchment to remove them from the pan before slicing into squares. To store, wrap individually with plastic wrap or pack in an airtight container.

Ivy

FALL

HARVEST DINNER | ANNUAL PIE NIGHT
SOUP BAR | AUTUMN EVENING AT HOME

HARVEST DINNER

ON THE MENU

ESSENTIAL ROASTED TURKEY

AUTUMN SWEET POTATO SALAD

GOLDEN CRESCENT ROLLS

BROWN BUTTER GREEN BEANS WITH CRUNCHY BREADCRUMBS

GRUYÈRE BRIOCHE STUFFING

My first time hosting Thanksgiving dinner was on the patio of the small apartment Syd and I rented as newlyweds, with a table set for two using a leftover tablecloth from our wedding. While my skills have improved with time and practice, it has always been one of my favorite holidays. Unlike other celebrations, there's no pressure to exchange gifts, only a shared intention to connect, enjoy good food, and give thanks. Whether I'm hosting two or ten, the hours before Thanksgiving always look the same—the dining table is set, serving platters selected, and flowers arranged. Meanwhile, the kitchen buzzes with the chaos of timers beeping, dishes stacking, and someone asking where the serving spoons went.

I want a formal table to feel luxurious but never overdone. In this scene, I layered toile napkins, mixed metals, and sprawling florals in vivid autumnal tones. The menu is my take on the classics: an essential roasted turkey infused with aromatics, a shaved Brussels sprouts salad tossed with maple vinaigrette and sweet potatoes, green beans under a blanket of brown butter and breadcrumbs, and a brioche stuffing made rich with Gruyère. Whether you're hosting the big day or selecting a recipe or two to bring to Friendsgiving, by the end of the night, the platters will be picked clean, the stories a little louder, and the laughter easy.

STYLING: *To give a tablescape the attention it deserves, I set it up the day before and make a list to do as much prep work as possible.*

Wren
Menu
Essential Roasted Turkey
Sweet Potato Salad
Golden Crescent Rolls
Brown Butter Green Beans
with Crunchy Breadcrumbs
Gruyère Brioche Stuffing

YIELD: 10–12 SERVINGS PREP: 45 MIN REST: 26 HR COOK: 3 HR 15 MIN

ESSENTIAL ROASTED TURKEY

For many years now, I have roasted our family's Thanksgiving turkey. After much trial and error, I've fine-tuned my recipe: a savory dry rub and plenty of herbs and aromatics. It's the most flavorful turkey I've ever had. Better yet, the drippings make a silky gravy that you'll want to pour over absolutely everything.

INGREDIENTS

TURKEY & POTATOES

1 cup kosher salt
1 cup firmly packed light brown sugar
4 tablespoons dried rubbed sage
8 teaspoons ground mustard powder
4 teaspoons freshly cracked black pepper
4 teaspoons onion powder
4 teaspoons garlic powder
2 teaspoons ground nutmeg
1 (12- to 15-pound) turkey, thawed
5 pounds baby potatoes, such as red or Yukon Gold
1 yellow onion
1 navel orange
1 bunch fresh thyme
¾ cup unsalted butter, melted, divided
Orange and fresh rosemary, for garnish

MUST-HAVE GRAVY

½ cup unsalted butter
1 garlic clove
½ cup all-purpose flour
¼ teaspoon ground nutmeg
3 to 4 fresh thyme or rosemary sprigs
4 cups turkey or chicken stock
1 to 1½ cups turkey drippings

TIP: Roast the turkey with potatoes (as written) to simplify dinner, or remove the potatoes entirely and bake the turkey solo.

DIRECTIONS

Prepare the Turkey

1. Make the dry brine by combining the salt, brown sugar, sage, mustard powder, pepper, onion powder, garlic powder, and nutmeg.

2. Pat the turkey dry on all sides and set it on the rack of a 16- or 18-inch roasting pan. Generously rub the dry brine onto the turkey, working it underneath the skin and over every part of the bird, including inside the cavity. Depending on the size of your bird, you may not need all of the rub. If any rub falls off the turkey, leave it in the bottom of the pan. Discard any unused rub.

3. Refrigerate the turkey, uncovered, for at least 24 hours and up to 48 hours.

4. About 1 hour before roasting, remove the turkey from the fridge and let rest at room temperature. Preheat the oven to 400 degrees and position the rack in the bottom third of the oven.

5. Pat the turkey dry, leaving as much of the dry brine on the bird as possible. Quarter the onion and orange, then stuff them inside the cavity of the turkey along with the thyme. Truss the turkey. To do so, use a skewer to cinch the loose neck skin closed, tuck the wings beneath the breast, and use twine to tie the turkey's back legs together.

6. Lift the trussed turkey and rack out of the roasting pan. Add the baby potatoes to any juices the turkey left behind in the bottom of the pan, then nestle the turkey and rack over the potatoes. Using a pastry brush, coat the entire turkey in ½ cup of the melted butter. Pour any extra butter over the potatoes.

Continued on next page →

7. Roast the turkey and potatoes, uncovered, for 30 minutes, rotating the pan halfway through. Remove the turkey from the oven, leaving the door cracked, and reduce the heat to 300 degrees. Cover the turkey with aluminum foil and return to the oven, closing the oven door.

8. Roast for 1 hour 45 minutes to 2 hours 15 minutes, depending on the size of your bird. Once the turkey's internal temperature reaches 150 to 155 degrees, remove the foil and brush with the remaining ¼ cup melted butter. Roast for an additional 30 minutes, uncovered, or until the internal temperature reaches 165 degrees.

9. Let the turkey and potatoes rest, covered with aluminum foil, for 30 minutes before carving.

10. Reserve the drippings. Pour the drippings through a fine-mesh sieve into a heat-proof bowl or large measuring cup. This removes any browned bits, skin, or herbs, leaving you with a smooth base for your gravy.

Make the Gravy

11. In a small saucepan melt the butter over medium heat. Mince or grate the garlic, then add it and the flour to the pan. Whisk frequently for 5 to 7 minutes, or until the flour smells nutty and begins to darken. Add the nutmeg, thyme or rosemary sprigs, and stock.

12. Increase the heat to high and bring the gravy to a boil. Whisk constantly until the gravy is viscous and thick, coating the back of a spoon. Add 1 cup of the turkey drippings and whisk to combine. Taste the gravy and add more drippings, if desired. Remove the thyme or rosemary sprigs and serve the gravy alongside the turkey and potatoes.

YIELD: 12 SERVINGS PREP: 45 MIN COOK: 43 MIN

AUTUMN SWEET POTATO SALAD

This is a robust fall salad made with all the good stuff—shaved Brussels sprouts, sweet potatoes, smoky bacon, maple pecans, and chewy dried cranberries. Tossed with an orange vinaigrette, it's all the flavor and color you expect during the holidays, scooped onto your fork.

INGREDIENTS

MAPLE CITRUS VINAIGRETTE

⅓ cup extra-virgin olive oil
1 teaspoon Dijon mustard
1 tablespoon maple syrup
⅛ teaspoon cayenne pepper
½ teaspoon kosher salt
½ shallot
1 navel orange

SALAD & ASSEMBLY

2 sweet potatoes (about 2 pounds), peeled
1 tablespoon extra-virgin olive oil
1 teaspoon kosher salt, divided
3 tablespoons unsalted butter
4½ teaspoons maple syrup
1 teaspoon ground cinnamon
1½ cups pecan halves
1½ pounds fresh Brussels sprouts
1 cup dried cranberries
6 slices bacon, cooked

TIP: To save time, prepare the salad ingredients 1 to 2 days ahead of time and keep them refrigerated separately until ready to serve.

DIRECTIONS

1. Make the vinaigrette by adding the oil to a jar along with the mustard, maple syrup, cayenne, and salt. Whisk to combine. Mince the shallot, then zest the orange and juice it to yield about ¼ cup orange juice. Add the shallot, zest, and juice to the vinaigrette. Whisk to combine, then refrigerate until ready to serve.

2. Preheat the oven to 400 degrees. Dice the sweet potatoes into ½-inch cubes and toss with the oil and ½ teaspoon of the salt. Transfer the sweet potatoes to an 18 x 13-inch sheet pan, dividing them between two pans if needed to prevent overcrowding. Roast for 25 to 28 minutes until tender and slightly browned. Remove from the oven and allow to cool.

3. While the sweet potatoes roast, melt the butter in a medium heat-proof bowl. Add the maple syrup, cinnamon, and the remaining ½ teaspoon salt and whisk to combine. Add the pecans and toss to coat. Transfer to a sheet pan and toast in the oven for 12 to 15 minutes, or until the pecans smell nutty and look golden and sticky.

4. Shave the Brussels sprouts by using a mandoline or slicing as thinly as possible. Add to a serving bowl, then top with the roasted sweet potatoes, toasted pecans, and cranberries. Roughly chop the bacon and crumble it over the top. Dress the salad with the vinaigrette, then toss and serve.

YIELD: 32 ROLLS | PREP: 1 HR | REST: 1 HR 45 MIN | COOK: 20 MIN

GOLDEN CRESCENT ROLLS

It's not Thanksgiving without a crescent roll. My version is soft, buttery, and pillowy—just begging to be snatched off the pan and eaten warm. You'll find this dough referenced a few times because it's truly all-purpose and great for everything from Mini Cinnamon Rolls (pg. 257) to Basil Garlic Knots (pg. 85).

INGREDIENTS

ALL-PURPOSE DOUGH

5 cups (650 grams) all-purpose flour, fluffed, scooped, and leveled
⅓ cup (66 grams) granulated sugar
1 tablespoon (9 grams) fast-rising instant yeast
1½ teaspoons kosher salt
1 egg
⅓ cup (75 grams) neutral oil, such as avocado oil
⅓ cup (75 grams) water
1⅔ cups (378 grams) whole milk

ASSEMBLY

½ cup (113 grams) unsalted butter, softened
4 tablespoons (57 grams) unsalted butter, melted
Flaky salt, for serving

TIP: If you're new to making dough, this recipe is the perfect place to start.

DIRECTIONS

1. In the bowl of a stand mixer, add the flour, sugar, yeast, and salt. Whisk by hand to combine, then add the egg and the oil.

2. Combine the water and milk in a separate bowl or glass measuring cup, then microwave it in Brief increments until the mixture reaches 115 to 118 degrees (but no warmer). Pour the warm water and milk into the bowl, then return the bowl to the stand mixer fitted with a bread hook.

3. Knead the dough, starting on low speed and increasing to medium-high, for about 8 minutes total. The dough will look quite loose and feel tacky.

4. Remove the bowl from the stand mixer and scrape down the sides of the bowl with a rubber spatula. Cover the bowl with a clean towel, then set aside in a warm place to rise until doubled, 50 to 60 minutes. You'll know the dough is ready when you press it with your finger and the indent very slowly bounces back.

5. Line two 18 x 13-inch sheet pans with parchment paper. Use the rubber spatula to help release the dough from the bowl onto a floured work surface. The dough will be slightly tacky and sticky. Lightly dust the top of the dough with flour, then divide in half. One at a time, roll each half of dough into a 14-inch circle, then use an offset spatula to spread the softened butter over the surface. Slice each circle into quarters, then continue slicing each quarter into four triangles. The wide end of the triangles should be about 2 ½ to 3 inches wide.

6. Roll the triangles, starting at the wide end, to create a crescent shape. Transfer the crescents to the sheet pans, leaving about 2 inches of space between each roll.

Continued on next page →

7. Cover the pans loosely with plastic wrap and set aside in a warm place to rise until doubled, another 30 to 45 minutes. Meanwhile, preheat the oven to 350 degrees.

8. Remove the plastic wrap and transfer the risen rolls to the oven. You can bake both pans at the same time, rotating the pans halfway through baking. Bake for 18 to 20 minutes, or until the tops are golden brown. Remove from the oven and immediately brush with the melted butter and sprinkle with flaky salt.

YIELD: 10–12 SERVINGS PREP: 15 MIN COOK: 15 MIN

BROWN BUTTER GREEN BEANS WITH CRUNCHY BREADCRUMBS

My kids call these the "good green beans," and I must agree. They taste better than any green bean I've ever eaten. Steamed until tender yet snappy, they are tossed in a glossy brown butter sauce and served under a blanket of breadcrumbs. They might just be green beans, but they're always the star of the table.

INGREDIENTS

½ cup water
2 pounds fresh green beans, trimmed
3½ teaspoons kosher salt, divided
2 garlic cloves
½ cup unsalted butter
1½ teaspoons white wine vinegar
½ cup panko breadcrumbs

DIRECTIONS

1. In a large skillet bring the water to a simmer over medium-high heat. Add the green beans and 3 teaspoons of the salt, then immediately cover and reduce the heat to medium. Let the green beans steam for 5 to 7 minutes until bright green and al dente. Drain off any extra water, then transfer the green beans to a serving platter.

2. Return the pan to the stove over medium-low heat. Thinly slice the garlic and chop the butter into tablespoon-size pieces. Add the butter to the pan and once melted, add the garlic. Continue cooking the butter and garlic for about 3 minutes, watching closely, until the butter is deeply browned and smells nutty.

3. Remove the pan from the heat and add the white wine vinegar. Whisk to combine, then pour the sauce over the green beans.

4. In the same pan use the residual browned butter to toast the panko. Place the pan back on medium heat, then add the panko and the remaining ½ teaspoon salt. Stir frequently until golden, 3 to 4 minutes. Sprinkle the breadcrumbs over the green beans and serve immediately.

TIP: Make the breadcrumbs ahead of time by browning 1 tablespoon butter over medium heat, then toasting the panko for 3 to 4 minutes. Store in an airtight container at room temperature.

YIELD: 12 SERVINGS PREP: 35 MIN COOK: 2 HR 50 MIN

GRUYÈRE BRIOCHE STUFFING

This stuffing sits at our table year after year. The flavor is complex from jammy caramelized onions and grated Gruyère, yet still nostalgic thanks to a mix of fresh sage, rosemary, and thyme. Don't rush the process—trust that every moment spent caramelizing the onions is well worth your time.

INGREDIENTS

¾ cup unsalted butter, plus more for greasing the pan
1½ pounds brioche
3 medium yellow onions
4 stalks celery
3 tablespoons fresh sage leaves
3 tablespoons fresh thyme leaves
4½ teaspoons fresh rosemary leaves
3¾ cups chicken or turkey stock
3 eggs
1 egg yolk
2½ teaspoons kosher salt
3 cups grated Gruyère

DIRECTIONS

1. Preheat the oven to 300 degrees and lightly butter a 13 x 9-inch casserole dish.

2. Tear the brioche into approximately 1-inch pieces and place on an 18 x 13-inch sheet pan, using two pans if needed to keep the bread in a single layer. Toast the bread for 35 to 40 minutes until crusty like a crouton, then let cool slightly.

3. While the bread toasts, thinly slice the onions from pole to pole and slice the celery in ¼-inch pieces. Add the butter to a large skillet over medium-low heat. Once melted, add the onions and celery and cover. Stirring occasionally, cook for 50 to 60 minutes, until the onions are jammy and caramelized.

4. Increase the oven temperature to 350 degrees. About 10 minutes before the onions are done caramelizing, finely chop the sage, thyme, and rosemary. Add the herbs to the caramelized onions and stir to combine, then sauté for another minute until fragrant.

5. Add the stock to a large bowl. Add the eggs, egg yolk, and salt and whisk to combine.

6. Add the toasted brioche, caramelized onions, and grated Gruyère to the stock mixture. Toss until the bread is fully coated.

7. Transfer the stuffing to the prepared casserole dish. Cover the dish with aluminum foil and bake until the internal temperature reaches 165 degrees, 35 to 40 minutes. Remove the foil and cook uncovered for another 25 to 30 minutes, or until the top is browned.

ANNUAL PIE NIGHT

ON THE MENU

GUIDE TO CHARCUTERIE

RELIABLY FLAKY PIE CRUST

CHOCOLATE HAZELNUT MERINGUE PIE

PUMPKIN-PIE CHEESECAKE BARS

MIXED BERRY SLAB PIE

BROWN BUTTER PECAN PIE

Years ago, as my mom struggled to coordinate schedules for Thanksgiving dinner, she made an inspired decision—dessert first. Instead of juggling competing commitments, she invited everyone over the night before Thanksgiving, when calendars were lighter and guests were eager to indulge. With bellies not yet full of turkey and stuffing, pie night became a cherished tradition, an open-door evening for family and friends to gather around a kitchen island filled with flaky crusts, warm fillings, and decadent bites.

Now the baton has passed to me, and it's seventy-two hours straight of shuffling between the sink, range, and refrigerator preparing to host both pie night and Thanksgiving dinner. Believe it or not, it's one of the highlights of my year. Classic pies like pecan and mixed berry mingle with my personal favorite, chocolate hazelnut meringue, and thick pumpkin cheesecake bars. Pies sit alongside charcuterie boards overflowing with savory meats, ribbons of carefully arranged crackers, cheeses, and a wheel of Brie drizzled with honey. Our annual pie night always reminds me why I love entertaining. It's straightforward to plan, full of beloved recipes, and always better when shared with the people you love.

STYLING: *When styling a charcuterie board, start by placing the cheeses followed by stacks of crackers and meats in different shapes and colors. Fill in the gaps with nuts and groupings of fruit. Garnish with fresh herbs.*

GUIDE TO CHARCUTERIE

Pie night or otherwise, a cheese board is commonly on the table when I'm hosting. Fan crackers and sliced fruit, pile candied nuts to create texture, and experiment with slicing or breaking apart cheeses to add interest. This way the board is abundant and becomes a welcome invitation for grazing.

INGREDIENTS

1 to 2 soft cheeses, such as goat cheese, Brie, or Roquefort
1 to 2 hard cheeses, such as Gruyère, Manchego, or Mimolette
1 sweet spread, such as honeycomb, honey, or jam
1 cup pickles or mixed olives
3 cured meats, such as Calabrese salami, prosciutto, hard salami, or Capicola
3 to 4 cracker types, such as seeded toasts or water crackers
2 to 3 fresh fruits, such as grapes, pears, apples, or pomegranates
2 to 3 roasted or candied nuts, such as candied pecans, pistachios, or toasted walnuts
Fresh herbs, for styling

DIRECTIONS

1. Anchor your board with the cheeses. Set them equal distance apart in slices, as whole wheels or wedges, or with a few crumbles removed with a cheese knife.

2. Place 1 to 2 small bowls of spreads or olives in the empty spaces. If using something like honeycomb, put it directly on the board near a cheese knife.

3. Fold or drape the cured meat near the cheese, organizing them into piles or sweeping lines.

4. Add stacks, piles, or fans of crackers around the board, keeping them near the meat and cheeses.

5. Slice fruit such as apples or pears, then arrange them around the board. You won't need a lot to make the board look abundant; just focus on creating shapes through bundles, fans, or pieces of fruit (like pomegranate) rustically cracked open.

6. Finally, fill any empty spaces with piles of nuts. Tuck fresh herbs around the perimeter of the board, letting them spill over the edges. Serve within 1 to 2 hours of preparing.

TIP: Add a variety of flavor and texture profiles. I like to choose a spicy cured meat like Calabrese salami to pair with mellow varieties. With cheeses, I always choose an herby variety for color and freshness.

YIELD: 2 ROUNDS OR 1 SLAB PREP: 30 MIN REST: 30 MIN

RELIABLY FLAKY PIE CRUST

After many frustrating attempts in my early days of pie making, I found that shortening and butter is the magic combination. With the flavor of butter and the forgiveness of shortening, this crust is extremely approachable and equally tender and flaky.

INGREDIENTS

- 1 cup (226 grams) unsalted butter, cold
- ¾ cup (138 grams) vegetable shortening
- 3⅓ cups (433 grams) all-purpose flour, fluffed, scooped, and leveled
- 1½ teaspoons kosher salt
- 2 tablespoons (25 grams) granulated sugar
- 1 tablespoon (14 grams) white vinegar
- ¾ cup (170 grams) cold water

TIP: For long-term storage, wrap the dough tightly with plastic wrap and freeze for 2 to 3 months.

DIRECTIONS

1. Slice the butter into ½-inch pieces. Measure the shortening, then keep both the butter and shortening in the fridge until ready to use.

2. To the bowl of a food processor, add the flour, salt, and sugar. Pulse a few times to combine.

3. Add the chilled butter and shortening to the food processor. In 1-second increments, pulse the mixture 13 to 15 times. There should be a variety of butter sizes, none larger than a pebble. Transfer the mixture to a medium bowl and add the white vinegar.

4. Measure the cold water, then add a few ice cubes. Being careful not to get any ice in the dough, gradually pour some of the water over the flour mixture and use a fork to toss the mixture together. Stop adding water when the dough is supple, but not tacky or wet. You may not use all of the water.

5. Continue tossing to create a shaggy dough, then use your hands to briefly bring the dough together inside the bowl.

6. Transfer the dough to a lightly floured work surface. If preparing the dough for 9-inch pie plates, divide the dough in two and form each into a round. Alternatively, leave the dough in one piece and form it into a rough slab.

7. Cut one round (or the single slab) into quarters. Working quickly, stack the quarters on top of each other and press down. Form into a round (or rectangle) again, then repeat 2 to 3 times. Wrap the dough tightly with plastic wrap and refrigerate. Repeat this same process with the second round of dough, if applicable.

8. Refrigerate for at least 30 minutes (and up to 72 hours) before rolling and plating.

YIELD: 8 SERVINGS PREP: 40 MIN COOK: 40 MIN REST: 4 HR

CHOCOLATE HAZELNUT MERINGUE PIE

My grandma is my muse for all things comfort food. Every year she made a silky chocolate pie topped with a glorious pile of meringue. This is my twist on her recipe, made with a hazelnut crust and chocolate hazelnut filling. Every time I take a bite, I think of her—which only makes me love this pie more.

INGREDIENTS

GRAHAM CRACKER HAZELNUT CRUST

10 rectangular graham cracker sheets (155 grams)
½ cup (71 grams) hazelnuts
¼ cup (50 grams) granulated sugar
1 teaspoon kosher salt
6 tablespoons (85 grams) unsalted butter, melted

CHOCOLATE HAZELNUT FILLING

½ cup (71 grams) hazelnuts
¾ cup (149 grams) granulated sugar, divided
⅔ cup (113 grams) milk chocolate chips
2 cups (454 grams) whole milk
4 egg yolks, whites reserved for meringue
⅓ cup (37 grams) cornstarch
1 tablespoon (14 grams) vanilla extract
¼ cup (21 grams) unsweetened cocoa powder
½ teaspoon kosher salt

MERINGUE

4 egg whites, cold
¼ teaspoon cream of tartar
¾ cup (149 grams) granulated sugar
¼ cup (57 grams) water

TIP: Pressing the custard through the mesh sieve takes strong muscles and patience, but it is worth the extra effort for a silky pie.

DIRECTIONS

Prepare the Crust

1. Preheat the oven to 350 degrees, then add the graham crackers, hazelnuts, sugar, and salt to a food processor. Process into a sandy powder, 15 to 20 seconds. Add the melted butter and pulse until the mixture resembles wet sand and begins to clump.

2. Using the bottom of a drinking glass or measuring cup, press the mixture into a deep-dish 9-inch pie plate. Pack the crust down on the bottom and sides, then transfer to the oven and bake until set, 10 to 12 minutes. Remove from the oven and increase the oven temperature to 375 degrees.

Make the Chocolate Filling

3. In the same food processor, add the hazelnuts and ¼ cup (50 grams) of the sugar. Process continuously, scraping the sides of the bowl halfway through, for 2 to 3 minutes. The mixture should resemble sandy clay.

4. Add the chocolate chips to a medium bowl with a fine-mesh sieve placed over the top. Set aside.

5. In a medium saucepan whisk the milk, egg yolks, cornstarch, vanilla, cocoa powder, salt, hazelnut-sugar mixture, and the remaining ½ cup (99 grams) sugar until completely combined. Set over medium heat, then whisk constantly. First the mixture will steam, then it will simmer, and then it will thicken quickly. As soon as the mixture simmers and begins thickening, whisk constantly and vigorously for another 90 seconds.

6. Remove the custard from the heat and use a spatula to press it through the fine-mesh sieve into the bowl. This is a labor of love—it may take some work, but keep going, and don't forget to scrape the bottom of the sieve when done. Whisk to combine the melted chocolate with the custard, then set aside.

Continued on next page →

Meringue & Assembly

7. In the bowl of a stand mixer fitted with a whisk attachment, add the egg whites, cream of tartar, and a generous pinch of salt. Whisk the mixture on medium speed for 5 to 6 minutes until soft peaks form.

8. In a saucepan over medium heat, add the sugar and the water. Use a wet pastry brush or paper towel to wipe the edges of the pan completely clean. Without ever stirring the sugar mixture, let it come to a simmer. Once simmering, continue cooking for 3 to 4 minutes (again, without stirring) until the mixture reaches 240 degrees.

9. Increase the mixer speed to medium-high and, while mixing, very slowly pour the hot sugar mixture into the bowl in a thin stream. Continue beating on medium-high speed for 7 to 8 minutes until the egg whites reach a stiff peak.

10. Now, assemble the pie. Transfer the chocolate filling to the graham cracker crust, then add the meringue on top. Use a spatula to spread the meringue over the entire pie, making sure to cover all of the chocolate filling. Make swoops in the meringue using the spatula or the back of a spoon.

11. Bake the pie in the oven for 18 to 20 minutes, or until the top of the meringue is deeply browned. Let the pie rest at room temperature for at least 2 hours, then wrap loosely with plastic wrap and refrigerate for an additional 2 hours prior to serving.

YIELD: 16 BARS | PREP: 25 MIN | COOK: 1 HR 20 MIN | REST: 6 HR

PUMPKIN-PIE CHEESECAKE BARS

Pumpkin pie is good, but pumpkin pie with cheesecake is a dessert I can really get behind. These bars use shortbread to mimic pie crust and are topped with swirls of pumpkin pie and cheesecake fillings. Let them cool slowly for a smooth top, but even with a few cracks these bars are still beautiful.

INGREDIENTS

SHORTBREAD CRUST

2 ¼ cups (293 grams) all-purpose flour, fluffed, scooped, and leveled
¼ cup (50 grams) granulated sugar
1 teaspoon kosher salt
¾ cup (170 grams) unsalted butter, melted

CHEESECAKE BASE

3 (8-ounce) blocks (672 grams) full-fat cream cheese, room temperature
¾ cup (149 grams) granulated sugar
½ cup (107 grams) firmly packed light brown sugar
½ teaspoon kosher salt
3 eggs, room temperature
1 tablespoon (14 grams) vanilla extract
¼ cup (57 grams) heavy whipping cream, room temperature

PUMPKIN PIE FILLING

1 (15-ounce) can (425 grams) pumpkin puree
1 egg, room temperature
¼ cup (53 grams) firmly packed light brown sugar
½ teaspoon kosher salt
1 teaspoon ground cinnamon
¾ teaspoon ground ginger
¼ teaspoon ground cloves
¼ teaspoon ground nutmeg

DIRECTIONS

1. Preheat the oven to 350 degrees. Make the shortbread by combining the flour, sugar, and salt in a medium bowl. Pour the melted butter over the top, then toss together with a fork until the mixture is clumpy but combined. Press the crust into a 13 x 9-inch cake pan, then bake for 23 to 25 minutes until set and the crust is matte.

2. While the crust bakes, make the cheesecake base. Add the cream cheese, granulated sugar, brown sugar, and salt to the bowl of a stand mixer fitted with a paddle attachment. Beat on medium speed for 5 minutes until airy and smooth. Even if the mixture looks smooth a few minutes into mixing, keep going for the full time to incorporate more air. This results in a light and fluffy cheesecake.

3. Add the eggs one at a time, beating for a full 60 seconds between each addition. Finally, add the vanilla and cream and mix until just combined.

4. In a medium bowl, whisk together the pumpkin puree, egg, sugar, salt, cinnamon, ginger, cloves, and nutmeg until well combined. Set aside.

5. Once the shortbread is finished (no need to cool), reduce the oven temperature to 325 degrees. Pour the cheesecake base onto the crust, spreading in an even layer. Dollop the pumpkin pie filling over the top, then use a skewer to swirl the pumpkin into the cheesecake base. Do this until there is a good mix of large pockets of pumpkin and wispy, marbled threads.

6. Bake the bars for 50 to 55 minutes, or until the sides are set, the center jiggles like Jell-O, and the edges are golden brown. The bars will continue to set as they cool. Let rest at room temperature until cooled, 1 to 2 hours, then transfer to the fridge and chill for at least 4 hours or overnight. Slice and enjoy.

YIELD: 12 SERVINGS PREP: 1 HR 15 MIN COOK: 45 MIN

MIXED BERRY SLAB PIE

My yearly antiquing trips to Round Top, Texas, are never complete without a visit to Royers for junkberry pie. While this recipe isn't a copy, it was certainly inspired by their iconic mix of jammy berries. With an ideal crust-to-filling ratio, serve this pie warm out of the oven with a scoop of ice cream.

INGREDIENTS

1 Honeycrisp apple, skin on
1 pound strawberries
1 pint blueberries
1 pint blackberries
1 pint raspberries
1 lemon
¾ cup (149 grams) granulated sugar
¼ cup (53 grams) firmly packed light brown sugar
¾ teaspoon kosher salt
⅓ cup (37 grams) cornstarch
2 batches Reliably Flaky Pie Crust (pg. 201)
1 egg
1 tablespoon (14 grams) heavy whipping cream
Turbinado sugar, for sprinkling

TIP: Make the filling 3 to 4 days ahead of time and refrigerate until ready to use. Additionally, you can drape the pie crust into the pan, cover with plastic, and refrigerate for 2 to 3 days ahead of time.

DIRECTIONS

1. First, prepare the mixed berry filling. Core and shred the apple using a box grater, then roughly chop the strawberries. Add the shredded apple, chopped strawberries, and whole blueberries, blackberries, and raspberries to a large pot. Juice the lemon and add 2 tablespoons (28 grams) of the juice to the pot.

2. Set the pot over medium-high heat and add the granulated sugar, brown sugar, and salt. Use a spatula to stir the berries frequently and bring the mixture to a boil. Once boiling, cook for 5 to 6 minutes, and use the spatula to mash the berries.

3. Reduce the heat to low, then remove about 1 cup of the berry mixture with a liquid measuring cup. Add the cornstarch to the berries in the measuring cup, then whisk to combine. Pour the berry and cornstarch slurry back into the pot and stir well.

4. Cook, stirring vigorously, for another 2 to 3 minutes. Remove the berries from the heat and let cool completely. To speed the process, transfer the berries to a shallow bowl and stir often.

5. Meanwhile, prepare the crust. On a lightly floured work surface, roll one full recipe of Reliably Flaky Pie Crust into a 20 x 28-inch rectangle.

6. Transfer the dough to an 18 x 13-inch sheet pan, then trim away any dough that extends more than 1 inch over the edge. Tuck the remaining dough underneath itself, all around the perimeter of the pan. Refrigerate while preparing the second crust.

7. Take the second Reliably Flaky Pie Crust recipe and roll into another 28 x 20-inch rectangle. Trim any ragged edges to create a clean rectangle. Then, working lengthwise, slice the dough into long 1-inch strips.

Continued on next page →

8. Transfer the cooled berry filling to the refrigerated pie crust and spread evenly over the bottom. Using the strips of pie dough, begin to lattice them over the top of the filling. Start in the center with a strip of pie dough extending from one corner to another. Leave an equal space between each strip of dough and continue adding them until you fill the sheet pan.

9. Now, working the opposite direction, add another layer of pie dough strips. Alternate placing them over or behind the existing dough strips to create a lattice.

10. Trim the overhanging dough strips just long enough to tuck underneath the edges. Crimp the edges using your fingers, then transfer to the fridge and preheat the oven to 400 degrees.

11. Prepare an egg wash by whisking together the egg and the cream. Using a pastry brush, brush the egg wash over the pie dough and sprinkle with the turbinado sugar.

12. Transfer the pie to the oven and bake until the crust is golden, 30 to 32 minutes. Slice the pie and serve warm with scoops of Salted Vanilla Bean Ice Cream (pg. 159).

YIELD: 8 SERVINGS PREP: 30 MIN REST: 4 HR COOK: 1 HR 48 MIN

BROWN BUTTER PECAN PIE

It's not pie night without a pecan pie. This is my no-fuss recipe, made with the magic of brown butter (which, to no one's surprise, is a favorite ingredient of mine). The result is a familiar but complex flavor, making it a quintessential Southern classic with just a little bit of flair.

INGREDIENTS

- 1 round Reliably Flaky Pie Crust (pg. 201)
- 3 cups (315 grams) pecan halves
- ¾ cup (170 grams) unsalted butter
- 1 cup (312 grams) light corn syrup
- 1 cup (213 grams) firmly packed light brown sugar
- 1 teaspoon kosher salt
- 6 eggs, divided
- 1 tablespoon (14 grams) water

TIP: Make the pecan filling 2 to 3 days ahead of time and store in an airtight container in the fridge. Additionally, you can blind-bake the pie crust up to 1 day ahead of time.

DIRECTIONS

1. On a lightly floured work surface, roll the pie dough into a circle 12 inches in diameter. To make sure the dough is large enough, flip a 9-inch pie plate (preferably deep-dish) upside down and set it in the center of the rolled dough. The dough should extend about 1 inch beyond the edges of the pie plate.

2. Transfer the dough to the pie plate, letting it naturally drape into the plate. Trim any excess dough that hangs more than 1 inch from the sides, then tuck the remaining dough underneath itself. Crimp the edges and place in the refrigerator for at least 30 minutes.

3. To a large skillet over medium heat, add the pecan halves. Toast, tossing the pecans frequently, until lightly browned with a nutty aroma, 7 to 10 minutes. Remove the pecans from the skillet and let cool.

4. To the same skillet add the butter. Set over medium heat and cook, stirring only occasionally, until the butter browns. It will bubble and froth and will eventually smell like toffee with streaks of golden brown emerging through the foam. This takes 6 to 7 minutes. Immediately remove the butter from the heat.

5. To a large bowl add the corn syrup and brown sugar. Pour the warm butter over the top, then whisk to combine. The mixture will be smooth, homogenous, and a bit oily.

6. Add the salt and 5 of the eggs, one at a time, whisking to combine between each addition. Next, finely chop about half of the toasted pecans. Add both the chopped and whole pecans to the egg mixture and stir to combine. Refrigerate until ready to use.

Continued on next page →

7. Preheat the oven to 425 degrees. Remove the pie crust from the fridge, line with parchment paper, and add pie weights or dry beans, filling the crust at least halfway up the sides.

8. Transfer the pie crust to the oven and blind-bake for 16 to 18 minutes, or until the edges are light brown and the bottom of the crust is set. While the crust bakes, whisk together the remaining egg and the water.

9. Remove the pie weights and parchment, then brush the bottom and sides with the egg wash. Do not prick the crust. Immediately transfer the crust back to the oven without pie weights and bake 2 to 3 minutes to set the egg wash. Remove from the oven, then reduce the oven temperature to 350 degrees.

10. Stir the pie filling well to recombine, then pour it into the crust. Transfer the pie back to the oven and bake for 40 minutes. Remove the pie from the oven and cover with aluminum foil, then return to the oven and continue baking for 25 to 30 minutes or until the edges are set, the center of the pie jiggles like Jell-O, and the internal temperature reads 195 to 200 degrees.

11. Let the pie rest at room temperature for 2 hours to cool. Transfer the pie to the fridge and chill for at least 2 hours or until ready to serve.

Start

SOUP BAR

ON THE MENU

CHICKEN TORTILLA SOUP

ROASTED RED PEPPER & TORTELLINI SOUP

CAULIFLOWER CORN CHOWDER

BEEF POT PIE SOUP

TURKEY & WILD RICE SOUP

CORNBREAD BUNDTS WITH ROSEMARY HONEY BUTTER

When the leaves turn amber and the evenings grow cooler, I find myself instinctively reaching for my largest Dutch oven and favorite wooden spoons. This time of year is rooted in memories of simmering pots, the coziness of a bustling kitchen, and the nourishment of hot soup. A soup bar is perfectly suited for potluck-style gatherings without too many surprises. I'll usually make two soups, prepare toppings, and bake my cornbread bundts (slathered generously with rosemary honey butter), then ask friends to bring along one pot of their most-loved recipe. As the host, I plan by setting out coordinated tureens, pots, and ladles, so the evening feels cohesive even though the concept is laid-back.

Whether it's ladling out bowls of my chicken tortilla soup with homemade broth, or savoring a spoonful of red pepper tortellini soup piled high with freshly grated Parmigiano-Reggiano, the potluck feels like a gathering of stories—rich, layered, and deeply comforting.

STYLING: *Set up tureens and coordinating copper pots for serving before guests arrive to create cohesion out of the collection of recipes.*

YIELD: 6 SERVINGS PREP: 35 MIN COOK: 1 HR 40 MIN

CHICKEN TORTILLA SOUP

If you feel intimidated by cooking with a whole chicken, this soup is a great place to start. Just lower the chicken into the water and let it simmer for about an hour. The resulting broth is intensely satisfying, a perfect base for shredded chicken, chewy hominy, and a smattering of toppings.

INGREDIENTS

CHICKEN TORTILLA SOUP

1 yellow onion
2 poblano peppers
3 garlic cloves
3 tablespoons extra-virgin olive oil
4½ teaspoons dried Mexican oregano
1 tablespoon ground cumin
2½ teaspoons chili powder
2 tablespoons kosher salt
12 cups (3 quarts) water
1 (3½- to 4-pound) whole chicken
1 (15-ounce) can black beans, drained and rinsed
1 (15-ounce) can white hominy, drained and rinsed

TOPPINGS

2 limes
2 avocados
2 radishes
1 bunch cilantro
¾ cup sour cream
6 ounces tortilla chips

DIRECTIONS

1. Chop the onion and poblanos, then thinly slice the garlic. Add the oil to a 6- to 8-quart capacity stockpot and warm over medium heat. Sauté the onion, poblano, and garlic for 3 to 4 minutes, or until beginning to soften.

2. Add the oregano, cumin, chili powder, and salt. Cook for another 1 to 2 minutes, stirring constantly, until the spices are fragrant.

3. Next, add the water and bring to a boil. Immediately reduce the heat to low, then add the whole chicken. Cover the pot and cook at a bare simmer until the chicken is cooked through and very tender, at least 60 minutes and up to 75 minutes. The internal temperature of the chicken should reach at least 165 degrees, but will likely be higher. Using a spoon, occasionally skim fat that rises to the top.

4. Remove the chicken from the pot. Allow it to cool slightly, then remove the skin and shred the meat. Return the shredded chicken to the pot, then add the black beans and hominy. Bring to a simmer and cook for an additional 10 to 15 minutes.

5. Just before serving, slice the limes into wedges, dice the avocados, slice the radishes, and roughly chop the cilantro. Serve each bowl of soup with a wedge of lime, then top with avocado, radishes, cilantro, dollops of sour cream, and tortilla chips.

YIELD: 6 SERVINGS PREP: 10 MIN COOK: 20 MIN

ROASTED RED PEPPER & TORTELLINI SOUP

The key to making a great weeknight soup is a delicious broth. This recipe uses roasted peppers and heavy whipping cream, blended until smooth to create a tangy, sweet base for whole basil leaves, crumbled sausage, and cheese tortellini. It's easy and comforting—a perfect bookend to the day.

INGREDIENTS

1 pound Italian sausage
4 garlic cloves
5 ounces fresh spinach
1 cup fresh basil leaves, packed
2 tablespoons tomato paste
10 cups chicken stock, divided
1 (16-ounce) jar roasted red peppers, drained
1 pound cheese tortellini
½ cup heavy whipping cream
Grated Parmigiano-Reggiano, for serving

DIRECTIONS

1. Preheat a heavy-bottomed Dutch oven over medium-high heat. Crumble the sausage into the pot and leave undisturbed for 2 to 3 minutes to develop a caramelized crust. Stir the sausage and continue cooking until no longer pink, 3 to 4 minutes. Use a slotted spoon to remove the sausage from the pot, leaving behind the fat. Reduce the heat to medium-low.

2. Mince or press the garlic and add it to the pot, then add the spinach and basil. Cook for 2 to 3 minutes to wilt the spinach and basil, stirring constantly to prevent the garlic from burning.

3. Add the tomato paste and cook for about 1 minute. Slowly add 8 cups of the chicken stock, scraping up any browned bits at the bottom of the pot. Bring to a simmer.

4. While the soup simmers, add the roasted red peppers and 1 cup of the chicken stock to a blender and blend until completely smooth. Add the blended peppers to the Dutch oven and stir to combine. Increase the heat to high and bring to a boil.

5. Add the tortellini and cook according to package directions. Reduce the heat to medium, then return the sausage to the pot. Add the cream and stir to combine. If needed, add the remaining 1 cup chicken stock to achieve desired consistency. Serve with Parmigiano-Reggiano.

YIELD: 6 SERVINGS | PREP: 30 MIN | COOK: 45 MIN

CAULIFLOWER CORN CHOWDER

Chowder is always in my soup rotation, and this is the one I turn to again and again. It's simultaneously cozy and fresh, loaded with cauliflower and kernels of sun-kissed corn. This soup is best made in late summer or fall, when the corn is ripe and bursting with sweetness.

INGREDIENTS

4 ears corn, shucked and trimmed
2 ½ pounds cauliflower
2 leeks
4 ounces pancetta
4 teaspoons kosher salt
4 cups (1 quart) water
1 ½ cups whole milk
1 cup mascarpone
¼ cup minced fresh chives, plus more for garnish

DIRECTIONS

1. Slice the corn kernels from the cobs, then set the kernels aside and keep the cobs. Break the cauliflower down into florets. Finally, halve the leeks lengthwise, thoroughly wash them, and chop the whites and tender greens into ¼-inch pieces.

2. Off the heat, add the pancetta to a Dutch oven. Place the pot over medium heat and brown the pancetta, stirring frequently, for 6 to 7 minutes or until crisp. Using a slotted spoon, remove the pancetta from the pot, leaving behind the drippings.

3. Add the leeks and cauliflower to the pot. Sauté until the leeks begin to caramelize and the cauliflower begins to soften and brown slightly, 5 to 7 minutes. Add the salt.

4. Place the corn cobs in the pot and add the water. Bring to a boil, then immediately reduce the heat to low and cover. Simmer for 18 to 20 minutes, until the broth is fragrant and flavorful and the cauliflower is soft but not mushy.

5. Remove the corn cobs from the soup and discard. Add the milk, then use an immersion blender to blend about ⅓ of the soup. Finally, add the corn kernels and simmer for another 8 to 10 minutes until the corn is tender and the soup has barely reduced.

6. Take the pot off the heat and stir the mascarpone and chives into the soup. Divide the chowder between bowls and top with pancetta and more chives for garnish.

TIP: Make this soup any time of year with 3 cups of frozen corn and 1 quart of veggie broth in place of the corn cobs and water.

YIELD: 6 SERVINGS PREP: 50 MIN COOK: 2 HR 35 MIN

BEEF POT PIE SOUP

A few years ago, Syd and I celebrated our anniversary in the Cotswolds. On a drizzly evening at a quaint restaurant in the countryside, we had a beef pot pie that I will never forget. This stew, with fall-apart braised beef and herbaceous puff pastry croutons, is my way of revisiting that evening over and over.

INGREDIENTS

BEEF POT PIE SOUP

1 (2 ½- to 3-pound) chuck roast
⅓ cup all-purpose flour
4 ½ teaspoons kosher salt, divided
1 teaspoon freshly cracked black pepper
1 yellow onion
4 medium carrots
5 tablespoons neutral oil, such as avocado oil, divided
1 tablespoon tomato paste
1 tablespoon herbes de Provence
1 ¼ cups stout beer, such as Guinness
8 cups (2 quarts) beef stock
2 sprigs fresh rosemary
½ pound yellow potatoes
½ pound green beans, trimmed
1 tablespoon apple cider vinegar

HERBES DE PROVENCE CROUTONS

1 egg
1 tablespoon water
2 sheets frozen puff pastry, thawed
Herbes de Provence, for sprinkling
Flaky salt, for sprinkling

DIRECTIONS

1. Cube the roast into 1-inch pieces. Add to a large bowl and toss with the flour, 4 teaspoons of the salt, and pepper. Set aside to rest. Meanwhile, chop the onion into ½-inch pieces and thinly slice the carrots.

2. Add 4 tablespoons of the oil to a large Dutch oven and warm over medium-high heat. Once the oil is rippling, work in two batches to sear the meat, reserving any excess flour at the bottom of the bowl. Sear each batch for 5 to 6 minutes, flipping the meat halfway through. Once at least two sides of the beef are browned, remove them from the pot and set aside. Sprinkle any excess flour over the top of the seared beef.

3. Reduce the heat to medium, then add the remaining 1 tablespoon oil along with the chopped onion and carrots. Cook for 5 minutes, stirring frequently, until the onions begin to soften. Add the tomato paste and herbes de Provence, sautéing for another 30 seconds to 1 minute, until the tomato paste begins to caramelize and the herbes de Provence is fragrant.

4. Slowly add the stout, scraping up any browned bits on the bottom of the pot. Add the beef stock, then increase the heat to high and bring to a boil. Immediately reduce the heat to low, then return the seared meat to the pot. Add the rosemary sprigs and the remaining ½ teaspoon salt, then cover the pot and let simmer on the lowest setting for 1 ½ hours, stirring occasionally.

5. After the soup is done simmering, dice the potatoes into ½-inch cubes and chop the green beans into 1-inch pieces. Add to the pot and continue simmering, uncovered, for an additional 30 minutes.

6. Meanwhile, make the puff pastry croutons. Preheat the oven to 375 degrees, then whisk together the egg and water until no

Continued on next page →

streaks remain. Brush the egg wash over the puff pastry sheets. Sprinkle all over with herbes de Provence and flaky salt.

7. Line two 18 x 13-inch sheet pans with parchment paper. Cut the puff pastry into 1-inch squares, then transfer them to the sheet pans and bake for 12 to 14 minutes until puffed and golden. Let cool, then remove them from the pans.

8. To finish the soup, remove and discard the rosemary sprigs, add the apple cider vinegar, and stir to combine. Serve heaping ladles of soup topped with a handful of puff pastry croutons.

YIELD: 8 SERVINGS PREP: 35 MIN COOK: 1 HR

TURKEY & WILD RICE SOUP

Seasoned with thyme and ginger, these turkey meatballs are exceptionally good on their own. When added to a nourishing soup of squash, kale, and wild rice, they somehow become even more flavorful. It's a relatively easy soup and one I turn to repeatedly during the fall months.

INGREDIENTS

1 egg
⅔ cup panko breadcrumbs
1 tablespoon fresh thyme leaves
½ teaspoon freshly cracked black pepper, plus more for serving
7 teaspoons kosher salt, divided
1-inch knob fresh ginger, divided
1 pound ground turkey
1 shallot
1½ pounds butternut squash
5 cups curly-leaf kale, stems removed
8 ounces cremini mushrooms
3 tablespoons extra-virgin olive oil, divided
8 cups (2 quarts) turkey or chicken stock
1 bundle fresh thyme (about 8 to 10 sprigs)
1 cup wild rice, uncooked
1 lemon

TIP: If making the soup ahead of time, cook the wild rice separately and add it to the soup just before serving. This prevents the rice from soaking up too much of the liquid.

DIRECTIONS

1. First, make the meatballs. In a large bowl whisk the egg until no streaks remain. Add the panko, thyme leaves, pepper, and 2 ½ teaspoons of the salt. Grate half of the ginger into the mixture. Stir to combine. Finally, add the ground turkey and mix.

2. Coat your hands in olive oil to prevent sticking, then form the mixture into 2-tablespoon-sized balls. Set aside.

3. Finely chop the shallot and grate the remaining ginger. Peel, deseed, and dice the butternut squash and set it aside in a large bowl. Chop the kale and slice the mushrooms, then set aside separately.

4. Warm 2 tablespoons of the oil in a Dutch oven over medium-high heat. Add the meatballs and cook for 3 to 4 minutes, then gently turn them and cook for an additional 3 to 4 minutes to brown the other side. Once two sides of the meatballs are golden brown, remove them from the pot. They won't be cooked through.

5. Reduce the heat to medium-low. Add the remaining tablespoon oil to the pot, followed by the shallots and the remaining ginger. Cook, stirring frequently, for 2 to 3 minutes.

6. Slowly add the stock, scraping up any browned bits on the bottom of the pot. Add the thyme sprigs and the remaining 4 ½ teaspoons salt, then increase the heat to high and bring to a boil. Rinse the wild rice and add it to the pot along with the squash. Reduce the heat to low, then cover and simmer for 20 minutes.

7. Return the meatballs to the pot, then add the kale and mushrooms. Continue simmering for another 15 minutes until the meatballs are cooked through and the rice is tender. Squeeze the lemon into the soup and serve each bowl with an extra crack of black pepper.

YIELD: 16–18 BUNDTS PREP: 25 MIN COOK: 15 MIN

CORNBREAD BUNDTS WITH ROSEMARY HONEY BUTTER

This cornbread is sweet with a moist, cake-like texture. Sure, you could make it in a big pan and serve it in slices—but is there a better (or cuter) way to entertain than with individual bundts? Serve them in a big bowl next to whipped rosemary honey butter and watch as they quickly disappear into hungry hands.

INGREDIENTS

CORNBREAD

½ cup (113 grams) unsalted butter
¼ cup (84 grams) honey
¾ cup (149 grams) granulated sugar
2 eggs, room temperature
1½ cups (341 grams) buttermilk, room temperature
1 cup (138 grams) cornmeal
1 cup (130 grams) all-purpose flour, fluffed, scooped, and leveled
1 tablespoon (12 grams) baking powder
1½ teaspoons kosher salt
1 tablespoon (4 grams) minced fresh rosemary leaves

ROSEMARY HONEY BUTTER

1 cup (226 grams) unsalted butter, softened
2 tablespoons (8 grams) minced fresh rosemary leaves
2 tablespoons (42 grams) honey
2 tablespoons (28 grams) heavy whipping cream
½ teaspoon kosher salt

TIP: If you don't have a mini bundt pan, a muffin tin works just as well.

DIRECTIONS

1. Place a mini bundt pan in the oven and preheat to 375 degrees. Meanwhile, melt the butter and let it cool.

2. In a medium bowl whisk together the honey, sugar, eggs, and buttermilk until fully combined. Add the melted butter and whisk.

3. In a large bowl combine the cornmeal, flour, baking powder, salt, and rosemary. Add the buttermilk mixture to the cornmeal mixture, whisking until just combined. It's okay if there are a few lumps.

4. Remove the bundt pan from the oven and, working quickly, spray the pan with cooking spray and add the batter to each bundt. You will use about ¼ cup batter per mold, depending on the size of the pan.

5. Bake the cornbread for 13 to 14 minutes or until the tops are browned along the edges. Let the cornbread cool in the bundt pan, then remove each bundt by inserting a knife and gently lifting out.

6. While the cornbread cools, make the whipped butter. Add the butter, rosemary, honey, cream, and salt to the bowl of a stand mixer fitted with a whisk attachment. Start on low speed and slowly increase to medium speed, whipping the butter until it's light and airy. Serve the butter alongside the cornbread.

FRENCH COUNTRY COOKING

AUTUMN EVENING AT HOME

ON THE MENU

BUTTERNUT SQUASH ENCHILADAS
CRUNCHY CABBAGE SLAW
MAGIC CRISPY BARS

In Utah we are blessed with four distinct seasons, and our tastes tend to change with the temperature. After months spent outside enjoying the garden and lighter fare, this is the season I start to cook differently. We move indoors. I roast more. I reach for deeper flavors, a little more spice, and a little more warmth.

This is the dinner for making a Tuesday night feel special or hosting a casual evening with friends. The butternut squash enchiladas are a hearty main dish that leans into fall with a smoky sauce of blistered vegetables. It's paired with a crunchy cabbage slaw tossed in a Cumin Lime Vinaigrette that cuts through the robustness of the enchiladas with acidity and texture. To finish the meal, I've included a playful, no-bake twist on two of my favorite childhood treats—crisped rice bars layered with toasted coconut, pretzels, and just the right hit of chocolate and butterscotch.

STYLING: *A handful of fresh herbs has a way of pulling everything together—adding a final touch that makes any dish feel more refined and complete.*

Monika Hibbs
Gather at Home
THE KINFOLK GARDEN

BUTTERNUT SQUASH ENCHILADAS

When I have a little extra time, these enchiladas are on the menu. The roasted butternut squash is seasonal, and it creates a dreamy enchilada sauce when blended with blistered tomatoes, onion, and jalapeños. Make sure to serve these enchiladas with a generous helping of Crunchy Cabbage Slaw (pg. 243).

INGREDIENTS

2 pounds butternut squash
3 tablespoons extra-virgin olive oil, divided
3 teaspoons kosher salt, divided
½ pound tomatillos
½ pound Roma tomatoes (about 2 tomatoes)
1 jalapeño
½ yellow onion
2 garlic cloves
1½ pounds chicken breast, boneless and skinless
4 teaspoons chili powder
2 teaspoons ground cumin
⅛ teaspoon ground cloves
1¼ cup chicken stock, divided
14 to 16 corn tortillas
1 (15-ounce) can black beans, drained and rinsed
4 cups grated Oaxaca or mozzarella
Cilantro, for serving
Radishes, for serving
Sour cream, for serving

TIP: To make the enchiladas mild, only use half of the deseeded jalapeño. To make the enchiladas spicier, don't deseed the jalapeño and/or use two.

DIRECTIONS

1. Preheat the oven to 475 degrees. Peel, deseed, and dice the squash into 1-inch cubes. Place the squash on an 18 x 13-inch sheet pan and toss with 1 tablespoon of the oil and 1 teaspoon of the salt.

2. Remove the papery husks of the tomatillos by soaking them in hot water for 10 seconds, then sliding the husks off. Dry the tomatillos. Place the whole tomatillos, tomatoes, and jalapeño (no need to remove the stem) on a second sheet pan. Peel and slice the onion into four wedges, then smash and peel the garlic. Add to the sheet pan, leaving room in the center for the chicken.

3. Pound or butterfly the chicken breasts until they are approximately 1 inch thick. Combine the chili powder, cumin, ground cloves, and the remaining 2 teaspoons salt. Rub the spice mixture over the chicken to coat, then place the chicken on the sheet pan and drizzle with the remaining 2 tablespoons oil.

4. Transfer both sheet pans to the oven, placing the pan with the chicken on the rack above the sweet potatoes. Roast for 12 to 14 minutes, then remove the chicken from the pan (its internal temperature should be 165 degrees). Continue roasting all of the vegetables for 10 minutes, until the squash is tender and the other vegetables are charred. Remove the sheet pan from the oven and reduce the oven temperature to 350 degrees.

5. Shred the chicken using forks or a stand mixer and set aside. Transfer the roasted squash to a food processor or blender and add ¼ cup of the chicken stock. Blend until smooth, scraping the sides as needed. Remove about two-thirds of the squash puree and set aside to use during assembly.

6. Next, make the enchilada sauce. To the blender with the remaining squash, add the roasted tomatillos. Pull the stem off

Continued on next page →

the jalapeño and deseed it, then use your hands to peel the skin off the tomatoes (which should be effortless). Add the tomatoes, jalapeño, onion, and garlic to the blender, along with any remaining juices on the pan. Finally, add the remaining 1 cup chicken stock and blend to combine. Taste the enchilada sauce and adjust for salt.

7. Add 1 ½ cups enchilada sauce to the bottom of a 13 x 9-inch pan. Char the tortillas over a gas burner, or warm them in a damp paper towel in the microwave. To each tortilla, add a heaping tablespoon of the reserved squash puree, shredded chicken, and black beans. Add a sprinkle of cheese, then roll the tortilla tightly and line up the enchiladas in the pan.

8. Pour the remaining enchilada sauce over the top and scatter with the remaining cheese. Cover the pan with aluminum foil and transfer to the oven. Bake for 30 minutes, then uncover the pan and turn on the broiler. Broil for 3 to 5 minutes, or until the cheese is browned and bubbling.

9. Serve the enchiladas with a sprinkle of cilantro, a few thin slices of the radishes, and a dollop of sour cream.

CRUNCHY CABBAGE SLAW

This slaw is more than the sum of its parts. After tossing a medley of crunchy vegetables with a smoky Cumin Lime Vinaigrette, serve it with Butternut Squash Enchiladas (pg. 239) or eat it as a standalone lunch.

INGREDIENTS

CABBAGE SLAW

½ head green cabbage, about 1½ pounds
½ head romaine
2 medium carrots
3 radishes
1 English cucumber
1 cup roasted peanuts

CUMIN LIME VINAIGRETTE

3 to 4 limes
½ cup extra-virgin olive oil
2 teaspoons ground cumin
¾ teaspoon chili powder
½ teaspoon granulated sugar
1 teaspoon kosher salt
1 garlic clove

DIRECTIONS

1. Shred the green cabbage and romaine and add to a large bowl. Cut the carrots and radishes into matchsticks (or grate them). Deseed the cucumber and slice it into matchsticks, then roughly chop the peanuts. Add the carrots, radishes, cucumber, and peanuts to the bowl with the greens. Toss to combine.

2. To make the vinaigrette, zest 1 lime and add the zest to a small bowl with the oil, cumin, chili powder, sugar, and salt. Juice the limes to yield approximately ⅓ cup juice, then grate or finely mince the garlic. Add the juice and garlic to the vinaigrette and whisk until smooth.

3. Pour the vinaigrette over the slaw and toss to combine.

YIELD: 12 BARS | PREP: 20 MIN | COOK: 10 MIN | REST: 2 HR

MAGIC CRISPY BARS

When I was growing up, my mom let me make two desserts without supervision: crispy rice treats and magic bars. This recipe combines both into a simple no-bake dessert that my kids love. Between the toasted coconut and the gooey sweetened condensed milk, these bars really are magical.

INGREDIENTS

- 1 cup (170 grams) butterscotch chips, plus more for serving
- 1 cup (170 grams) semisweet chocolate chips, plus more for serving
- ½ cup (113 grams) unsalted butter, plus more for greasing the pan
- 2 teaspoons vanilla extract
- ½ teaspoon kosher salt
- 1 (16-ounce) bag (450 grams) mini marshmallows
- ¾ cup (234 grams) sweetened condensed milk
- 6 cups (180 grams) puffed rice cereal
- 1½ cups (105 grams) crushed pretzels
- 2 cups (106 grams) unsweetened shredded coconut flakes

DIRECTIONS

1. Place the butterscotch chips and chocolate chips in the freezer, then generously butter a 13 x 9-inch pan and set aside. In a large Dutch oven, melt the butter over medium-low heat until sizzling and starting to foam. Remove from heat.

2. Immediately add the vanilla, salt, and marshmallows and stir constantly until the marshmallows are almost completely melted. Pour in the sweetened condensed milk and stir to combine.

3. Add the rice cereal and crushed pretzels and fold the mixture gently to combine. Set the Dutch oven aside to cool for 8 to 10 minutes. Meanwhile, lightly toast the coconut in a large skillet over medium-low heat until fragrant and just beginning to turn golden brown—about 5 minutes. Set aside a few tablespoons of toasted coconut, then add the rest to the Dutch oven along with the frozen butterscotch and chocolate chips. Fold the mixture quickly and very gently to avoid melting the chips. Stop stirring as soon as the chips are incorporated.

4. Lightly press the bars into the prepared pan, making sure not to pack them down too tightly in order to maintain a fluffy, light texture. Sprinkle with additional chips and the reserved coconut, then let cool for at least 2 hours before slicing and serving.

TIP: This recipe moves quickly. To set yourself up for success, prepare all the ingredients before starting.

Ivy

WINTER

CHRISTMAS MORNING | COOKIE EXCHANGE
HOLIDAY DINNER PARTY | DATE NIGHT

CHRISTMAS MORNING

ON THE MENU

SAVORY DUTCH BABY
MINI CINNAMON ROLLS
CITRUS & FENNEL SALAD

After the presents were unwrapped and paper covered the floor, my brother and I would press our faces to the oven glass to see if the Dutch baby had puffed. Made from a simple batter of eggs, flour, and milk, a Dutch baby is an impressive pancake with a custardy center and towering crisp edges. Its rustic texture and neutral flavor make it endlessly versatile—just as delicious with lemon and powdered sugar as it is with savory toppings like cheese, herbs, and greens.

I've carried this tradition into my own home, serving it straight from the skillet, which is both inviting and showstopping all at once. I like to set our table for Christmas dinner the night before, so we can make the most of the festive backdrop for breakfast as well. While I often serve the savory Dutch baby on its own, if you have time to complete the menu with mini cinnamon rolls and a vibrant citrus salad, please do. The cinnamon rolls were my solution to always wanting "just a bite," and the citrus and fennel salad glows like stained glass in the morning sun—a mix of blood oranges, beets, and pomegranate seeds layered with toasted hazelnuts and fennel fronds.

STYLING: *Investing in quality bakeware allows you to incorporate utility pieces as part of the aesthetic and serve straight from the pan without having to replate.*

LODGE

YIELD: 4–6 SERVINGS | PREP: 10 MIN | REST: 45 MIN | COOK: 20 MIN

SAVORY DUTCH BABY

My mom's go-to breakfast on Christmas was a Dutch baby. It's a fond memory—one I've passed on to my kids, who lovingly refer to this as "breakfast pizza." They aren't entirely wrong; it features a popover-like base topped with dollops of ricotta, a pile of arugula, and sweeping ribbons of prosciutto.

INGREDIENTS

1 tablespoon fresh thyme leaves
½ cup finely grated Parmigiano-Reggiano, plus more for serving
3 tablespoons minced fresh chives
4 eggs, room temperature
¾ cup all-purpose flour, fluffed, scooped, and leveled
¾ cup whole milk, room temperature
1 teaspoon kosher salt
2 tablespoons unsalted butter
4 ounces arugula
3 tablespoons lemon juice
1 cup whole-milk ricotta
2 ounces prosciutto
Flaky salt and freshly cracked black pepper, for serving

DIRECTIONS

1. Place a 10-inch cast-iron skillet into the oven and preheat it to 425 degrees. After the oven is at temperature, continue heating the pan for another 20 to 30 minutes.

2. Meanwhile, roughly chop the thyme leaves, and add them to a small bowl along with the Parmigiano-Reggiano and chives. Toss to combine.

3. Prep the Dutch baby batter by adding the eggs to a blender. Blend on medium speed for 1 to 2 minutes, or until the eggs are frothy and a pale butter yellow.

4. Add the flour, milk, and salt to the blender and blend until combined, about 1 minute. Set aside to rest at room temperature for at least 15 minutes and up to 30 minutes prior to baking.

5. Add the butter to the preheated skillet and leave in the oven until melted. Quickly blend the batter for another 10 to 15 seconds, then immediately pour the batter into the pan and sprinkle with the Parmigiano-Reggiano, thyme, and chives. Return it to the oven and bake until puffed, the edges are golden, and the center is cooked through—18 to 20 minutes.

6. While the Dutch baby bakes, toss the arugula with the lemon juice and a pinch of salt. Use a whisk to whip the ricotta, then tear the prosciutto in half.

7. Immediately after removing the Dutch baby from the oven, dollop with the ricotta and top with the dressed arugula, torn prosciutto, and a sprinkle of flaky salt and pepper. Serve immediately.

TIP: Make sure the oven and pan are extremely hot, don't overmix the batter, and be generous with the toppings.

YIELD: 48-50 MINI ROLLS PREP: 1 HR REST: 1 HR 45 MIN COOK: 30 MIN

MINI CINNAMON ROLLS

The Call family, a client from our *Dream Home Makeover* days, made us the most amazing cinnamon rolls. She sent us her recipe (handwritten with directions like "a pinch of this"), and with some careful tweaks, this recipe was born. My version is baked on a sheet pan in bite-size portions for snacking.

INGREDIENTS

CINNAMON ROLLS

- 1 recipe All-Purpose Dough (pg. 187)
- ¾ cup (170 grams) unsalted butter, softened
- ¾ cup (160 grams) firmly packed light brown sugar
- 2 tablespoons (15 grams) ground cinnamon
- 1 teaspoon kosher salt

MAPLE CREAM CHEESE FROSTING

- ½ cup (113 grams) unsalted butter, softened
- 1 (8-ounce) block (224 grams) full-fat cream cheese, softened
- 3 ¾ cups (450 grams) powdered sugar
- ¼ teaspoon kosher salt
- ¼ teaspoon ground cinnamon
- 2 tablespoons (39 grams) maple syrup

TIP: Spread the frosting over the cinnamon rolls while warm for a gooier glaze, or wait until they are completely cooled for a frosted roll.

DIRECTIONS

1. Prepare the All-Purpose Dough recipe (pg. 187) through step 4, transferring the dough to a large bowl for proofing. While the dough rises, butter an 18 x 13-inch sheet pan and set aside. Using a stand mixer with a paddle attachment, make the filling by whipping together the butter, brown sugar, cinnamon, and salt until smooth.

2. Use a rubber spatula to release the risen dough onto a lightly floured work surface. Divide the dough in half and roll each piece into a 27 x 8-inch rectangle.

3. Spread the filling from edge-to-edge over each rectangle. Starting at the long edge, roll the dough into a log. Pinch the seam closed and gently stretch the roll to make sure it's about 25 inches long.

4. Using a sharp knife or unflavored floss, cut the dough into 1-inch pieces. Each log will produce 24 to 26 cinnamon rolls.

5. Place the rolls ½ inch apart on the prepared sheet pan. One pan fits about 45 rolls, so put any extras on a second pan. Cover loosely and let rise until puffed and nearly doubled, 30 to 45 minutes.

6. Meanwhile, preheat the oven to 325 degrees. Bake the rolls for 25 to 30 minutes, or until the middle of the centermost cinnamon roll is 185 to 190 degrees.

7. While the rolls cool, make the frosting. To the bowl of a stand mixer fitted with a paddle attachment, add the butter, cream cheese, and powdered sugar. Mix for 2 to 3 minutes until smooth, starting on low and increasing to medium speed.

8. Add the salt, cinnamon, and maple syrup, then whip again on medium speed for 2 to 3 minutes until light and aerated. Frost the cinnamon rolls and serve.

YIELD: 8 SERVINGS PREP: 45 MIN COOK: 50 MIN

CITRUS & FENNEL SALAD

This salad celebrates winter's moody yet vibrant palette. Earthy steamed beets and citrusy blood oranges provide understated shades of maroon, while torn fennel fronds add verdant tones of green. It's an elegant blend of color, and it only feels right that it adorns a holiday breakfast table.

INGREDIENTS

1 pound medium beets
4 blood oranges
2 navel oranges
½ bulb fennel
¼ cup pomegranate juice
¼ cup extra-virgin olive oil
1 teaspoon honey
¾ teaspoon kosher salt
⅓ cup hazelnuts
¼ cup fennel fronds
¼ cup pomegranate arils

DIRECTIONS

1. Trim the beets by removing the stem and any long roots, then place them in a steamer basket over boiling water. Steam the whole beets for 35 to 45 minutes, depending on the size of the beets, until fork-tender. Set aside to cool.

2. While the beets are steaming, prep the blood and navel oranges. Use a knife to peel the rind and white pith off of each orange, then slice the oranges into coins about ¼ inch thick. Set on paper towels to drain off excess juice. Let rest while preparing the rest of the ingredients.

3. Thinly slice or shave the fennel bulb. Use a knife to peel the beets and slice into wedges no more than 1 inch thick.

4. Arrange the oranges on a serving platter, then top with the sliced fennel and beets.

5. Make the vinaigrette by whisking together the pomegranate juice, oil, honey, and salt. Pour the dressing over the salad.

6. Finally, roughly chop the hazelnuts and toast in a dry skillet over medium heat until fragrant and lightly browned, 4 to 5 minutes. Roughly chop or tear the fennel fronds over the salad, then sprinkle with the hazelnuts and pomegranate arils. Serve immediately.

TIP: To save time, prep the steamed beets a few days in advance, storing them in the refrigerator for 2 to 3 days prior to serving. Alternatively, you can use store-bought steamed beets.

bake

COOKIE EXCHANGE

ON THE MENU

CHOCOLATE PEPPERMINT SANDWICH COOKIES

SNOWBALL SANDIES

WHITE CHOCOLATE CHEWY GINGERSNAPS

COOKIE BUTTER BLOSSOMS

CREAM CHEESE SPRITZ WREATHS

TRIPLE-CHOCOLATE HOT CHOCOLATE

Cookies were my first foray into the kitchen. Every Sunday I'd climb up and perch beside the mixing bowl to help my mom make dessert. While the rest of the year felt like a week-by-week ritual, the holiday season was a true lesson in endurance. We baked cookies for friends, neighbors, family, and of course, ourselves. It was during those flour-dusted afternoons that I became a cookie connoisseur, and my mom, with admirable grace, learned patience.

Over the years my cookie list has only grown, blending beloved family traditions with new recipes I test and tweak each season. It's a tradition I now share with my own daughters, and many times, we have all three generations gathered in the kitchen, baking side by side. While I could have written an entire book about my love for cookies, I've narrowed it down to a few favorites—an assortment of flavors, shapes, and sizes designed to round out your holiday cookie tin.

STYLING: *For picture-perfect cookies, use a kitchen scale to weigh each portion of dough. Uniform sizing ensures consistency in baking and a more polished final presentation.*

YIELD: 40 SANDWICH COOKIES PREP: 45 MIN COOK: 20 MIN

CHOCOLATE PEPPERMINT SANDWICH COOKIES

There's a certain California-based grocery store with a seasonal peppermint sandwich cookie that is a mainstay of my winter pantry. This recipe is my soft and chewy rendition. Equally easy to make, enjoyable to eat, and festive in presentation, it's a cookie I would be thrilled to receive in any dessert box.

INGREDIENTS

CHOCOLATE COOKIES

½ cup (113 grams) unsalted butter, softened
½ cup (107 grams) firmly packed light brown sugar
½ cup (99 grams) granulated sugar
1 cup (170 grams) semisweet chocolate chips
1 egg, cold
½ cup (65 grams) all-purpose flour, fluffed, scooped, and leveled
½ cup (42 grams) Dutch-process cocoa powder
1 teaspoon baking soda
1 teaspoon kosher salt

PEPPERMINT FROSTING & ASSEMBLY

½ cup (113 grams) unsalted butter, softened
1¾ cups (210 grams) powdered sugar
½ teaspoon peppermint extract
½ teaspoon vanilla extract
¼ teaspoon kosher salt
6 candy canes (81 grams)
2 to 3 tablespoons (28 to 43 grams) whole milk

DIRECTIONS

1. Preheat the oven to 350 degrees. Line two 18 x 13-inch sheet pans with parchment paper and set aside. In the bowl of a stand mixer fitted with a paddle attachment, beat together the butter, brown sugar, and granulated sugar on medium speed for 4 to 5 minutes until light and fluffy. Scrape the sides of the bowl about halfway through.

2. Meanwhile, add the chocolate chips to a saucepan over medium heat and melt, stirring frequently. Once melted and smooth, remove from heat.

3. Add the egg to the creamed butter and sugar and mix on medium speed for about 30 seconds to 1 minute, scraping the sides of the bowl as needed. Pour the melted chocolate into the mixer and beat for another 30 seconds to combine.

4. In a separate bowl whisk together the flour, cocoa powder, baking soda, and salt. Add the flour mixture to the bowl of the stand mixer and, starting on low speed and progressively increasing to medium speed, beat until the cookie dough is completely combined. Be sure to scrape the sides of the bowl and the paddle to make sure everything is incorporated evenly.

5. Scoop dough by the tablespoon and place it onto each lined sheet pan about 1 ½ inches apart. Bake for 8 to 10 minutes. The cookies will spread, set, and crack over the top. Remove from the oven and let the cookies cool completely on the sheet pans before transferring them to a cooling rack. Repeat this process with the remaining cookie dough.

6. While the cookies cool, make the frosting. Wash and dry the stand mixer bowl and paddle, then add the butter, powdered sugar, peppermint extract, vanilla, and salt. Beat on medium speed until combined—the mixture will look light and creamy.

Continued on the next page →

7. Add the candy canes to the bowl of a food processor and process until they turn into a coarse, sandy texture. Add 1 tablespoon of the crushed candy canes to the frosting, then pour the rest onto a plate and set aside for decorating.

8. Lastly, add the milk to the frosting and mix to combine. Start with 2 tablespoons milk and add the third if needed to reach a spreadable consistency. Scrape the sides of the bowl, then beat again on medium speed until the frosting is airy, whipped, and smooth.

9. To assemble the cookies, spread one heaping tablespoon of frosting on the bottom of a cookie. Sandwich with another chocolate cookie, then roll the sides in the reserved crushed candy canes. Store in an airtight container at room temperature for 2 days, then wrap any extras with plastic wrap and refrigerate for another 1 to 2 days.

YIELD: 40–42 COOKIES PREP: 50 MIN COOK: 45 MIN

SNOWBALL SANDIES

In a crossover between pecan sandies and Mexican wedding cookies, these crescent moons are buttery, delicate, and profoundly nutty from a trio of toasted nuts. Shaped into sweet crescent moons, baked, and double-coated in powdered sugar, they are dreamy tea cookies that absolutely melt in your mouth.

INGREDIENTS

½ cup (64 grams) walnut halves
½ cup (53 grams) pecan halves
½ cup (75 grams) macadamia nuts
1 cup (226 grams) unsalted butter, room temperature
1⅓ cups (160 grams) powdered sugar, divided, plus more for dusting
½ teaspoon almond extract
2 cups (260 grams) all-purpose flour, fluffed, scooped, and leveled
1 teaspoon kosher salt

DIRECTIONS

1. Preheat the oven to 350 degrees and place the walnuts, pecans, and macadamia nuts on an unlined 18 x 13-inch sheet pan. Transfer to the oven and toast until the nuts are fragrant and beginning to develop a light brown color, 14 to 16 minutes. Remove from the oven and allow to cool.

2. Meanwhile, combine the butter, ⅔ cup (80 grams) of the powdered sugar, and almond extract in the bowl of a stand mixer fitted with a paddle attachment. Beat on medium speed for 3 to 4 minutes until light in color, scraping the sides of the bowl halfway through mixing.

3. Add the toasted nuts to a food processor and pulse until finely chopped. Add the flour and salt, then pulse a few more times to combine. Transfer the flour mixture to the stand mixer and mix for about 1 minute until no dry spots remain.

4. Line two 18 x 13-inch sheet pans with parchment paper. Scoop the dough into tablespoon-size balls. Use the palm of your hand to roll the balls into short cylinders about 2 inches long, then gently bend them into crescent shapes. Place the crescents 1 inch apart on the lined sheet pans.

5. Bake for 15 to 16 minutes, rotating the pans halfway through, until the edges are barely golden brown. While warm, toss the cookies in the remaining ⅔ cup (80 grams) powdered sugar. Let cool, then dust in a second layer of powdered sugar using a small sieve. Repeat this process with the remaining dough. Store cookies in an airtight container, separating layers of cookies with sheets of parchment paper, for 3 to 5 days.

YIELD: 20–22 COOKIES | PREP: 40 MIN | COOK: 14 MIN

WHITE CHOCOLATE CHEWY GINGERSNAPS

My interior style blends vintage with contemporary, and I sought to do the same with this cookie. The texture is chewy, much like an old-school gingersnap but with the new-school flair of orange zest, flaky salt, and an ivory draping of sweet white chocolate.

INGREDIENTS

1⅔ cups (217 grams) all-purpose flour, fluffed, scooped, and leveled
1 teaspoon baking soda
¾ teaspoon kosher salt
1 teaspoon ground cinnamon
1¾ teaspoons ground ginger
½ teaspoon allspice
¼ teaspoon ground nutmeg
¼ teaspoon espresso powder (optional)
½ cup (113 grams) unsalted butter, softened
⅓ cup (66 grams) granulated sugar
⅔ cup (142 grams) firmly packed light brown sugar
1 navel orange
¼ cup (85 grams) molasses

ASSEMBLY

1 tablespoon (7 grams) orange zest (reserved from the orange above)
1 tablespoon (4 grams) flaky salt
2 cups (360 grams) chopped white chocolate, or chips

DIRECTIONS

1. Preheat the oven to 350 degrees and line two 18 x 13-inch sheet pans with parchment paper. In a medium bowl whisk together the flour, baking soda, salt, cinnamon, ginger, allspice, nutmeg, and espresso powder (if using). Set aside.

2. To the bowl of a stand mixer fitted with a paddle attachment, add the butter, granulated sugar, and brown sugar and beat on medium speed for 4 to 5 minutes, until light and fluffy. Scrape the sides of the bowl about halfway through, making sure the butter and sugars are evenly combined.

3. Zest the orange. Reserve 1 teaspoon of zest for the dough, and 1 tablespoon of zest for the assembly. Juice the orange and measure 1 tablespoon (14 grams) of juice. Add the molasses, orange zest, and orange juice to the butter and sugar. Beat on medium speed for another 1 to 2 minutes to combine. Again, scrape the sides of the bowl about halfway through. Once finished beating, the mixture should look a bit lighter and airier.

4. Finally, add the flour mixture to the mixer. Starting on low speed and slowly increasing to medium, mix until the dry ingredients are fully incorporated into the dough.

5. Using a 2-tablespoon (30 grams) cookie scoop, place the cookie dough on the sheet pans, leaving about 2 inches between each ball of dough. Bake for 12 to 14 minutes, rotating the pans halfway through, until the cookies have spread and the sides are set.

6. Remove from the oven and let cool completely on the sheet pan. The cookies will be very soft at first, then firm up as they cool.

7. Once the cookies are cooled, add the tablespoon of orange zest to the flaky salt and toss with your fingers to combine.

Continued on next page →

8. Next, place a glass or metal bowl over a saucepan filled with 1 to 2 inches of water, making sure the bowl doesn't touch the water. Set the pan over medium heat and add the white chocolate to the bowl. Using a spatula, stir frequently. As soon as the water begins to simmer, reduce the heat all the way to low and continue stirring until the chocolate is completely melted. Turn off the heat but keep the saucepan and chocolate on the burner.

9. Dip half of each gingersnap into the melted white chocolate, then return to the cookies to the sheet pan or place on a cooling rack. Immediately sprinkle with a bit of the orange zest and salt, then let the cookies rest until the white chocolate is completely cooled and set. Store in an airtight container, separating layers of cookies with sheets of parchment paper, for 3 to 5 days.

YIELD: 40–42 COOKIES   PREP: 50 MIN   COOK: 14 MIN

COOKIE BUTTER BLOSSOMS

I make a new cookie each week in December, and last year I tested an update to a traditional peanut butter blossom. I have to say, I like it even better than the original. They are soft and barely spiced, with an added drizzle of cookie butter that keeps me going back for seconds (and thirds and fourths).

INGREDIENTS

- ¾ cup (170 grams) unsalted butter, slightly softened
- 1¼ cups (360 grams) creamy cookie butter, divided
- ¾ cup (149 grams) granulated sugar, divided
- 1 cup (213 grams) firmly packed light brown sugar
- 1 egg, cold
- 2 cups (260 grams) all-purpose flour, fluffed, scooped, and leveled
- ¼ teaspoon ground cinnamon
- 2 teaspoons baking powder
- 1 teaspoon kosher salt
- 42 Hershey's chocolate kisses, unwrapped

DIRECTIONS

1. Preheat the oven to 375 degrees. Line two 18 x 13-inch sheet pans with parchment paper. In the bowl of a stand mixer fitted with a paddle attachment, cream the butter, ¾ cup (216 grams) of the cookie butter, ¼ cup (50 grams) of the granulated sugar, and the brown sugar until pale, airy, and smooth—4 to 5 minutes on medium speed.

2. Scrape the sides of the bowl, then add the egg and beat for an additional 1 to 2 minutes. The mixture should look aerated and whipped.

3. To a separate bowl add the flour, cinnamon, baking powder, and salt, then whisk to combine. Add the flour mixture to the stand mixer and beat on medium speed until just combined. This should only take about 30 seconds.

4. Scoop the dough into tablespoon-size rounds, then roll them in the remaining ½ cup (99 grams) granulated sugar to coat. Place the cookies approximately 2 inches apart on the lined sheet pans and bake for 5 to 7 minutes, rotating the pans halfway through, or until the edges are just set.

5. While the cookies bake, warm the remaining ½ cup (144 grams) cookie butter in the microwave until thin and pourable, about 30 seconds.

6. After removing the cookies from the oven, work quickly to drizzle zigzags of melted cookie butter over the tops of the warm cookies. Finally, press a kiss into the center of each cookie. Let cool completely, then repeat this process with the remaining dough. To store, keep cookies in an airtight container at room temperature for up to 3 days.

YIELD: 125 COOKIES PREP: 1 HR COOK: 30 MIN

CREAM CHEESE SPRITZ WREATHS

A festive cookie with flecks of fresh cranberry and rosemary, these cookies are dangerous. They are petite and tangy with a slightly savory undertone, and you could eat an entire pan without realizing what you've done. Plus, my kids love using the spritz gun, which only adds to the fun.

INGREDIENTS

- 1 cup (198 grams) granulated sugar, divided
- ⅓ cup (33 grams) whole fresh or frozen cranberries
- 1 tablespoon (4 grams) roughly chopped fresh rosemary leaves
- ½ cup (113 grams) unsalted butter, slightly softened
- 4 ounces (112 grams) full-fat cream cheese, slightly softened
- 1 egg, cold
- 3 cups (390 grams) all-purpose flour, fluffed, scooped, and leveled
- ¾ teaspoon kosher salt

DIRECTIONS

1. Preheat the oven to 350 degrees and place two 18 x 13-inch sheet pans in the fridge (stacked is fine). Add ½ cup (99 grams) of the sugar, cranberries, and rosemary to the bowl of a food processor. Pulse until the cranberries and rosemary are blitzed into small pieces and the sugar resembles wet sand.

2. Transfer the cranberry sugar to the bowl of a stand mixer along with the remaining ½ cup (99 grams) sugar, butter, and cream cheese. Using a paddle attachment, beat the mixture for 4 to 5 minutes until light, airy, and smooth.

3. Add the egg and mix for 30 seconds to 1 minute, just until combined. Finally, add the flour and salt and mix, scraping the sides of the bowl as needed.

4. Transfer the dough to a cookie press fitted with a wreath stamp and remove the sheet pans from the fridge. Using a single pump for each cookie, press the spritz onto the sheet pans, fitting as many on each sheet as possible. These cookies don't spread much, so plan for 35 to 40 spritz cookies per sheet. Leave any remaining dough at room temperature.

5. Bake for 13 to 15 minutes, or until the cookies are set with a barely browned bottom. Let the cookies cool on the sheet pans, then use your hands to pop the cookies off the pan in a twisting motion. Transfer the sheet pans back to the fridge for 10 minutes, then repeat the pressing, baking, and cooling process with the remaining dough. Store the cookies in an airtight container for 5 to 7 days.

YIELD: 4 DRINKS PREP: 5 MIN COOK: 10 MIN

TRIPLE-CHOCOLATE HOT CHOCOLATE

A cup of thick, indulgent hot chocolate only seems right for the holidays. My version is a thoughtful blend of white, milk, and dark chocolate that's luxurious and salted without being too salty. Altogether, it's a dreamy sipping chocolate that tastes like drinking a smooth, milky ganache.

INGREDIENTS

1½ cups (341 grams) heavy whipping cream, divided
1 teaspoon vanilla extract
2 cups (454 grams) whole milk
1¼ cups (213 grams) white chocolate chips
⅔ cups (113 grams) milk chocolate chips
⅔ cup (113 grams) 70% dark chocolate chips
1½ teaspoons kosher salt
Shaved chocolate, for serving
Marshmallows, for serving (optional)

DIRECTIONS

1. To the bowl of a stand mixer, add 1 cup (227 grams) of the cream and the vanilla. Whip with a whisk attachment on medium speed until medium peaks form. Set aside for serving.

2. Add the milk and the remaining ½ cup (114 grams) cream to a saucepan over medium heat and whisk constantly. Once the milk begins to steam (do not bring to a boil), reduce the heat to low and add the white chocolate, milk chocolate, and dark chocolate chips.

3. Whisk slowly to combine the melting chocolate with the milk. Once the chocolate is nearly melted, remove the pan from the heat and add the salt. Continue whisking until smooth.

4. Serve the hot chocolate in mugs with a dollop of whipped cream, a fresh grating of chocolate, and a marshmallow (if using).

TIP: To serve the hot chocolate spiked, add 1½ ounces of white rum to your serving.

Wren

HOLIDAY DINNER PARTY

ON THE MENU

CRANBERRY BRAISED SHORT RIBS

CACIO E PEPE MASHED POTATOES

WINTER SALAD WITH TAHINI DRESSING

BROWN BUTTER CITRUS CAKE

Hosting a holiday dinner is the perfect excuse to embrace a little extra—a chance to dress up, pull out something that sparkles, and create an atmosphere that feels more lavish than the everyday. I'll dim the lights, set out place cards, and cue a festive playlist that sets the mood.

A deep crimson tablecloth is the dramatic backdrop to this table, draped with gathered silk ribbons and adorned with etched crystal. Lush florals in saturated burgundy and evergreen tones weave through the center of the table, echoing the warmth of the food and the intimacy of the gathering. At the heart of the menu is a showstopping platter of braised short ribs nestled into a bed of creamy mashed potatoes. The meat is caramelized and supremely tender, lacquered with a red wine reduction and accented by hearty carrots—comfort food elevated to special occasion status. A rustic winter kale salad adds contrast, flecked with sweet dates and toasted cornmeal breadcrumbs. Perched on a stand, a citrus cake is crowned with soft swirls of speckled brown butter frosting to complete the meal.

STYLING: *Tonal palettes make a striking statement on the table—here, we embraced a spectrum of rich red hues, layered through the linens, florals, and accents to create a look that feels both cohesive and bold.*

HIGH

YIELD: 6 SERVINGS PREP: 20 MIN COOK: 5 HR 15 MIN

CRANBERRY BRAISED SHORT RIBS

This recipe is a slow burn—comforting, fall-off-the-bone short ribs, submerged in red wine and cranberry juice, then braised for hours. Aside from looking beautiful before ever going into the oven, the best thing about this recipe is that you can prepare the rest of dinner while it braises.

INGREDIENTS

5 pounds beef short ribs, bone-in (6 to 8 ribs)
2 tablespoons kosher salt
1 garlic bulb
4 shallots
4 medium carrots
2 leeks
3 tablespoons neutral oil, such as avocado oil
2 tablespoons tomato paste
1 bunch fresh sage (about ½ cup packed)
1 cup whole fresh or frozen cranberries
3 cups pure cranberry juice
3 cups beef stock

DIRECTIONS

1. Preheat the oven to 325 degrees. Generously season the short ribs on all sides with the salt and set aside. While the meat rests, prepare the veggies. Slice the garlic bulb in half crosswise and roughly chop the shallots and carrots. Halve the leeks vertically, then clean the stalks and slice the white and tender green parts of the leeks into half-moons about ½ inch thick.

2. Add the oil to a large Dutch oven over medium heat. Once hot and the oil is just beginning to ripple, work in batches to sear the short ribs. Sear all sides until golden, flipping every 2 to 3 minutes, then remove from the pot.

3. Immediately add the garlic, shallots, carrots, and leeks to the Dutch oven and sauté for 6 to 8 minutes until beginning to soften. Add the tomato paste to the pot and cook, stirring constantly, until the tomato paste darkens and caramelizes against the bottom and sides of the pot, 2 to 3 minutes. Add the sage and cranberries.

4. Slowly pour in the cranberry juice and beef stock, using a wooden spoon or spatula to scrape up the fond on the bottom of the pot.

5. Nestle the short ribs into the Dutch oven, submerging them in the liquid, and bring to a bare simmer. Transfer the pot to the oven and braise, uncovered, for 4 to 4 ½ hours until the meat falls off the bone and shreds easily with a fork. Serve over Cacio e Pepe Mashed Potatoes (pg. 287).

YIELD: 10 SERVINGS PREP: 20 MIN COOK: 20 MIN

CACIO E PEPE MASHED POTATOES

These mashed potatoes are loaded with finely grated Pecorino Romano and copious amounts of pepper. It's a delicious twist on a traditional mash, capturing the flavor of cacao e pepe in a cloud of creamy potato. Serve with Cranberry Braised Short Ribs (pg. 285) or the Essential Roasted Turkey (pg. 181).

INGREDIENTS

- 5 pounds Yukon Gold potatoes
- 3 tablespoons plus 2½ teaspoons kosher salt, divided
- 1 lemon
- 4 tablespoons unsalted butter
- 1 cup finely grated Pecorino Romano, plus more for serving
- 2 teaspoons freshly cracked black pepper
- 1 cup heavy whipping cream
- 1½ cups whole milk

DIRECTIONS

1. Peel the potatoes and chop them into 1-inch pieces. Place the potatoes in a large pot or Dutch oven and fill with water, just to cover them. Add 3 tablespoons of the salt, then bring to a boil over high heat. While the potatoes cook, zest the lemon and measure 1 teaspoon of zest.

2. Once boiling, cook the potatoes for 18 to 20 minutes or until extremely tender. You should be able to poke a toothpick or fork all the way through the center of a potato with no resistance. Drain the potatoes and transfer them back to the pot, or to a stand mixer fitted with a whisk attachment, for mashing.

3. To the potatoes, add the lemon zest, butter, Pecorino Romano, pepper, cream, milk, and the remaining 2 ½ teaspoons salt. Mash the potatoes. If using the stand mixer, start on low speed until the liquid is incorporated into the potatoes, then increase to medium speed to whip until fluffy and mostly smooth, with just a few small lumps.

4. Serve with extra Pecorino Romano and top with Cranberry Braised Short Ribs (pg. 285). This recipe for mashed potatoes makes more than you might need and is plenty for heaping portions and some leftovers.

WINTER SALAD WITH TAHINI DRESSING

A salad dressed to the nines in deep greens, warm neutrals, and subtle golds is my kind of salad. The cornmeal breadcrumbs add a textural accent and much-needed crunch to complete the salad. Tahini dressing, peppered with fresh ginger and ground allspice, centers every bite.

INGREDIENTS

SEMOLINA BREADCRUMBS

1 cup semolina flour or finely ground cornmeal
2 tablespoons white sesame seeds
⅓ cup cold water
2 tablespoons extra-virgin olive oil
½ teaspoon kosher salt

GINGER TAHINI DRESSING

¼ cup tahini
¼ cup apple cider vinegar
1 teaspoon kosher salt
¼ teaspoon allspice
1-inch knob fresh ginger
3 tablespoons cold water

SALAD & ASSEMBLY

2 bunches Lacinato kale
½ head radicchio
2 Bosc pears
8 Medjool dates, pitted

DIRECTIONS

1. Preheat the oven to 450 degrees. In a medium bowl combine the semolina, sesame seeds, water, oil, and salt. The mixture will look a bit crumbly but will hold together if pressed. Transfer the mixture to an 18 x 13-inch sheet pan and break up any large pieces into smaller crumbs. Bake for 13 to 15 minutes, or until some of the crumbs turn irregular shades of golden brown. Remove from the oven and let cool.

2. Prepare the dressing by whisking together the tahini, vinegar, salt, and allspice in a small bowl. Grate the ginger into the vinaigrette, which will be very thick. Working one tablespoon at a time, slowly whisk in the water until you achieve a thin but viscous consistency.

3. Remove and discard the stems from the kale, then slice the leaves very thinly as if shredding them. Remove the core from the radicchio and slice it in the same fashion. Toss the kale and radicchio together in a large bowl or serving platter.

4. Core and cut the pears into ¼-inch-thick slices. Roughly chop the dates, then add both the pears and dates to the salad. If the dates are sticky, dampen your knife with water before chopping.

5. Toss the salad with the dressing to taste, then sprinkle all over with the breadcrumbs and serve immediately.

YIELD: 10 SLICES | PREP: 35 MIN | COOK: 55 MIN | REST: 2 HR

BROWN BUTTER CITRUS CAKE

Citrus is one of my most-used winter ingredients. This cake incorporates it all the way through, from its supple sponge to its stunning brown butter frosting. The frosting is a neutral, versatile backdrop for decorating—use grapefruit, berries, and any variety of greenery.

INGREDIENTS

CITRUS CAKE

- Unsalted butter, for greasing the pan
- 2 ¼ cups (293 grams) all-purpose flour, fluffed, scooped, and leveled
- 1 ¼ teaspoons baking powder
- ¼ teaspoon baking soda
- 1 teaspoon kosher salt
- 1 navel orange
- 1 medium grapefruit
- 1 cup (213 grams) firmly packed light brown sugar
- ¼ cup (50 grams) granulated sugar
- ¾ cup (170 grams) unsalted butter, melted
- 2 eggs, room temperature
- 2 egg whites, room temperature
- 1 cup (227 grams) whole milk

BROWN BUTTER FROSTING

- 1 cup (226 grams) unsalted butter
- 3 ¾ cups (450 grams) powdered sugar
- ½ teaspoon kosher salt
- 1 tablespoon (14 grams) vanilla extract
- 2 tablespoons (28 grams) orange or grapefruit juice
- ¼ cup (57 grams) heavy whipping cream

TIP: To suit any occasion, use fresh herbs, citrus, or other fruit to decorate the cake according to the event's color palette.

DIRECTIONS

1. Preheat the oven to 325 degrees. Grease an 8-inch cake pan with butter and line the bottom with a round of parchment paper. In a medium bowl whisk together the flour, baking powder, baking soda, and salt. Set aside.

2. Zest the orange and the grapefruit and measure 1 tablespoon (7 grams) zest from each. Juice either the orange or grapefruit for the frosting and measure 2 tablespoons (28 grams) of juice. Set the juice aside.

3. In the bowl of a stand mixer fitted with a paddle attachment, add the brown sugar, granulated sugar, melted butter, and orange and grapefruit zests. Cream on medium speed until very well combined, 3 to 4 minutes, scraping the sides of the bowl halfway through. The mixture should look whipped and pale.

4. Add the whole eggs, one at a time, mixing for about 30 seconds on medium speed between each addition to combine. Add both egg whites and mix again for another 30 seconds. Be sure to scrape the sides of the bowl and the paddle.

5. Heat the milk until very warm to the touch, 45 to 60 seconds in the microwave. Add half of the flour mixture and half of the warm milk to the stand mixer, then beat until just combined. Add the remaining flour mixture and warm milk, then beat again until just combined. Use a rubber spatula to scrape the sides of the bowl and the paddle, then stir again with the spatula to make sure everything is incorporated.

6. Pour the cake batter into the prepared cake pan and bake for 50 to 55 minutes until domed and golden brown. When done, a toothpick inserted into the center should come back with just a few moist crumbs, and the center will spring back when gently pressed. Transfer to a wire rack and cool completely, about 2 hours.

Continued on next page →

7. While the cake cools, prepare the brown butter frosting. Add the butter to a skillet over medium heat. Allow it to melt, then sizzle and foam, until streaks of golden brown emerge. Continue cooking for 6 to 7 minutes until the butter smells like toffee, stirring only occasionally to let it develop a dark, bronze color.

8. Remove from the heat. Transfer the brown butter to a bowl, making sure to scrape all the brown bits from the skillet, then cover with plastic wrap and refrigerate until the butter is the consistency of softened room temperature butter—20 to 30 minutes.

9. Add the brown butter, powdered sugar, and salt to the bowl of a stand mixer fitted with a paddle attachment. Mix on low speed until the frosting just begins to come together in a dry, crumbly mix. Add the vanilla and citrus juice, then mix again to combine. The frosting will look very thick.

10. Finally, add the cream and whip the frosting on medium speed for about 2 minutes until light in color, airy, and smooth.

11. Transfer the cake to a cake stand or plate, then frost. To store, place the cake under a cake dome or cover with plastic wrap and refrigerate for 3 to 5 days. Before serving from the fridge, let the cake come to room temperature.

DATE NIGHT

ON THE MENU

SILKY MASCARPONE PAPPARDELLE

CAESAR SALAD WITH CRISPY CHICKPEAS

CHERRY CHOCOLATE MOUSSE

POMEGRANATE SANGRIA

A date night for two is all about setting the mood and keeping things simple, prioritizing ease in the kitchen so you can be fully present at the table. For the styling, I lean into a "low and glow" approach, keeping florals and candlelight low to encourage connection and conversation across the table. The atmosphere should dance between luxurious and easygoing.

This menu offers a charming, elevated spin on comfort food, beginning with silky mascarpone pappardelle—broad, luxurious noodles wrapped in a velvety sauce with earthy shiitake mushrooms and spinach. It's paired with a light yet flavorful Caesar salad, where roasted chickpeas add crunch to little gem lettuce and a tangy, homemade dressing. To leave a lasting impression, cherry chocolate mousse (which is made ahead) is both decadent and airy. The meal is especially delicious when served with a glass of sparkling pomegranate sangria, a festive, jewel-toned sip that rounds out the evening.

STYLING: *When shopping for flowers at the supermarket, opt for bundles of a single variety to achieve a more polished, elegant look.*

YIELD: 2 SERVINGS PREP: 10 MIN COOK: 15 MIN

SILKY MASCARPONE PAPPARDELLE

With a surprising total of only six ingredients, this pappardelle is glossy and decadent. It balances earthy and sweet, with browned butter leaving behind caramelized flecks of gold. The only thing that makes this pasta better is laughter and easy conversation—luckily, Syd offers that in spades.

INGREDIENTS

8 ounces pappardelle
2 cups fresh baby spinach
4 ounces shiitake or cremini mushrooms
5 tablespoons unsalted butter, divided
½ cup mascarpone
Kosher salt, to taste

DIRECTIONS

1. Bring a large pot of heavily salted water to a boil, then cook the pasta until barely al dente according to package instructions. Before draining the pasta, reserve 2 cups of pasta water.
2. Meanwhile, finely chop the spinach and slice the mushrooms. To a large skillet over medium heat, add 1 tablespoon of the butter.
3. Once the butter is melted, add the mushrooms and let cook, stirring only once halfway through, for 6 minutes. Add the chopped spinach and cook for another 2 to 3 minutes, stirring frequently, until the spinach is completely wilted and no moisture remains.
4. Remove the mushrooms and spinach from the skillet and add the remaining 4 tablespoons butter. Cook the butter for 3 to 4 minutes until browned, then return the spinach and mushrooms to the pan. Add the mascarpone and stir to melt.
5. Add the pappardelle to the pan along with ¾ cup pasta water. Toss the pasta with the sauce and cook over medium-high heat for an additional 1 to 2 minutes until the sauce is glossy and slightly thickened. Add more pasta water if needed, then salt to taste and serve.

TIP: Turn this into an easy weeknight dinner for four by doubling the ingredients and cooking as directed.

YIELD: 4 SERVINGS PREP: 20 MIN COOK: 35 MIN

CAESAR SALAD WITH CRISPY CHICKPEAS

This is Caesar salad meets wedge salad, made with halves of artisan lettuce bathed in homemade dressing and topped with roasted chickpeas. The dressing is made with capers, keeping it vegetarian and offering a distinct, delightful tang. Top with a pile of Parmigiano-Reggiano—the more, the better.

INGREDIENTS

CAESAR DRESSING

2 lemons
½ cup mayonnaise
¼ teaspoon kosher salt
1 garlic clove
1½ teaspoons capers, drained
½ cup finely grated Parmigiano-Reggiano
Freshly cracked black pepper, to taste

CRUNCHY GARLIC CHICKPEAS & ASSEMBLY

1 (15-ounce) can chickpeas, drained, rinsed, and patted dry
1 tablespoon extra-virgin olive oil
1 teaspoon kosher salt
1 teaspoon garlic powder
2 heads Little Gem or artisan lettuce
Finely grated Parmigiano-Reggiano for serving

DIRECTIONS

1. Preheat the oven to 375 degrees. Juice the lemons and measure ¼ cup juice. Prep the dressing by combining the mayonnaise, lemon juice, and salt in a medium bowl.

2. Smash the garlic clove on a cutting board, then add the capers and a small pinch of salt. Mince the garlic and capers together, occasionally mashing with the side of your knife, until they almost resemble a paste. Add the garlic and caper mixture and the Parmigiano-Reggiano to the mayonnaise mixture. Whisk to combine. Add pepper to taste. Refrigerate until ready to use.

3. To a small bowl add the chickpeas, oil, salt, and garlic powder and toss to combine. Transfer the chickpeas to an 18 x 13-inch sheet pan and bake until golden and crisp, 32 to 34 minutes.

4. While the chickpeas cook, slice each head of lettuce in half lengthwise through the root. Wash the lettuce and let it drain cut-side down, patting gently with paper towels, until ready to serve.

5. To serve, place the lettuce halves on a platter cut-side up and generously top each wedge with dressing, crispy chickpeas, and more Parmigiano-Reggiano.

YIELD: 4 SERVINGS PREP: 20 MIN COOK: 5 MIN REST: 6 HR 30 MIN

CHERRY CHOCOLATE MOUSSE

Mousse is unmatched for us chocolate lovers. It's rich yet somehow light, and my version includes a substantial pour of Amarena cherry syrup for a touch of tartness. Use a high-quality chocolate—it's what makes the difference between a good mousse and a great one.

INGREDIENTS

1¼ cups (213 grams) chopped 72% dark chocolate
1½ cups (341 grams) heavy whipping cream, divided
⅓ cup (105 grams) Amarena cherry syrup
2 egg whites, cold
½ teaspoon kosher salt
⅓ cup (66 grams) granulated sugar
Amarena cherries, for serving
Finely grated chocolate, for serving

DIRECTIONS

1. Add 1 to 2 inches of water to a saucepan and set a heat-proof bowl over the top, making sure it doesn't touch the water. Add the chocolate, ½ cup (114 grams) of the cream, cherry syrup, and salt to the bowl.

2. Set the saucepan over medium-low heat and stir constantly until the chocolate melts into the cream and is almost completely smooth. This will take 3 to 4 minutes after the water begins steaming. Remove the bowl from the saucepan and set aside to cool for about 30 minutes.

3. To the bowl of a stand mixer fitted with a whisk attachment, add the egg whites. Whisk on medium-high speed for 9 to 10 minutes, gradually adding the sugar as the egg whites whip. Continue whipping until the egg whites reach medium peaks.

4. Gently fold about one third of the egg whites into the melted chocolate mixture, making sure to mix until no light or dark streaks remain. Add the remaining egg whites and gently fold until combined and no streaks remain.

5. Transfer the mousse to a small serving bowl and cover tightly with plastic wrap. Refrigerate for at least 6 hours, or up to overnight.

6. Just before serving, add the remaining 1 cup (227 grams) cream to a stand mixer fitted with a whisk attachment. Whip on medium speed until the whipped cream is airy and barely holds a peak, 3 to 4 minutes.

7. To serve, top a scoop of chocolate mousse with the unsweetened whipped cream, a few cherries, and finely grated chocolate.

YIELD: 6 DRINKS PREP: 20 MIN REST: 4 HR

POMEGRANATE SANGRIA

The beauty of sangria, among many things, is its "throw everything in a pitcher" mentality. This version is easygoing but sophisticated, with a touch of pomegranate for a wintry spin. Topped off with club soda for a hint of carbonation, it's a great cocktail to accompany dinner.

INGREDIENTS

2 Gala apples, skin on
2 navel oranges
½ cup pomegranate arils
1 (750-mL) bottle full-bodied dry wine, such as Cabernet Sauvignon
¼ cup brandy
1 cup pomegranate juice
1½ cups club soda, chilled

DIRECTIONS

1. Core and slice the apples into ¼-inch slices. Peel the oranges using a knife, making sure to remove any of the bitter white pith. Slice the oranges into rounds, then add the sliced apples, oranges, and pomegranate arils to a 4-quart pitcher.

2. Pour the wine, brandy, and pomegranate juice over the fruit. Gently stir, cover, and refrigerate for at least 4 hours or overnight.

3. When ready to serve, add the club soda and stir gently. Pour the sangria and enjoy.

TIP: To make a virgin sangria, use 3 cups pomegranate juice, 1 cup sweetened cranberry juice, and ½ cup apple juice or cider in place of the red wine and brandy.

WEEKNIGHT MEALS

Weeknight cooking often comes with a time limit, but that doesn't mean you have to sacrifice flavor, freshness, or intention. Just as a well-designed space can be both practical and beautiful, a thoughtfully prepared dinner can be both quick and deeply satisfying. In this chapter, I share a collection of recipes that come together in about an hour or less, built on whole ingredients and layered with vibrant, natural flavors—no bottled dressings or shortcuts required.

These meals are designed to fit into real life: a busy evening after work, a late soccer practice, or that moment when you're tempted to call for takeout. Instead, with a mix of fresh ingredients and a handful of pantry staples, you can create dishes that feel nourishing, unfussy, and grounded in good taste—where balance, contrast, and color come into play on the plate just as they do in a well-styled room.

YIELD: 6 SERVINGS | PREP: 25 MIN | COOK: 36 MIN

GARLICKY COD & QUINOA

While this is a quick sheet pan meal, it doesn't taste like you're cutting corners to get dinner on the table. The cod is delicate and flaky, topped with a garlic oil that is pronounced but not overwhelming. Roasted quinoa rounds out the meal and gets crispy at the edges for a nice crunch.

INGREDIENTS

- 8 garlic cloves
- ⅓ cup extra-virgin olive oil
- ½ teaspoon dried oregano
- 2 bunches broccolini (about 1 pound)
- 2 teaspoons kosher salt, divided
- 6 cups cooked quinoa, cooled
- 6 cod filets (4 to 6 ounces each)
- 1 tablespoon white wine vinegar

DIRECTIONS

1. Place either one 26 x 18-inch sheet pan or two 18 x 13-inch sheet pans in the oven and preheat to 450 degrees.

2. Thinly slice the garlic cloves, then add them to a small skillet along with the olive oil. Place the pan over medium-low heat until sizzling, then continue cooking until the garlic barely begins to brown—3 to 4 minutes. This will happen quickly, so watch the pan closely. Remove the pan from the heat, pour the garlic oil into a heat-safe bowl, and stir in the oregano.

3. Trim and discard the tough, stalky ends from the broccolini (about ½ inch from the bottom), then toss the broccolini with ½ teaspoon of the salt and 1 tablespoon of the prepared garlic oil, avoiding the garlic pieces if possible. Next, toss the quinoa with 3 tablespoons of the prepared garlic oil and another ½ teaspoon salt.

4. Remove the sheet pan(s) from the oven and, working quickly, transfer the quinoa onto the hot pan(s), dividing it evenly between the two if applicable. Top with the broccolini, then roast for 15 to 18 minutes until the quinoa turns golden at the edges and the broccolini is al dente. Reduce the oven temperature to 400 degrees.

5. Use 1 tablespoon of the prepared garlic oil and the remaining 1 teaspoon salt to season the cod filets, using your hands to slather them in the oil. Use a spatula to make room on the sheet pan for the filets, then add the fish. Roast until the cod is tender and flaky, 10 to 14 minutes (depending on the thickness of your cod) or until the fish reaches an internal temperature of 140 to 145 degrees.

6. Add the vinegar to the remaining garlic oil and stir to combine. Spoon the sauce over the roasted fish, then serve.

YIELD: 6 SERVINGS PREP: 15 MIN COOK: 20 MIN

BROCCOLI PISTACHIO SPAGHETTI

Whenever I need nourishment but want a big bowl of pasta, this is what I make. It's packed with broccoli and pistachios, which are scattered throughout the pasta like confetti. The best part is that the spaghetti is draped in a light, zippy sauce, made mostly of feta with a hefty splash of pasta water.

INGREDIENTS

1 shallot
¾ cup shelled pistachios, plus more for serving
1 (7-ounce) block feta
1 pound broccoli crowns or 10 ounces broccoli florets
1 pound spaghetti
2 tablespoons extra-virgin olive oil
Kosher salt, to taste

DIRECTIONS

1. Place a large pot of heavily salted water over high heat. While waiting for it to boil, finely chop the shallot, roughly chop the pistachios, and crumble the feta. Finally, trim the broccoli crowns into large florets and roughly chop the florets into small, bite-size pieces.

2. Once the water is boiling, add the spaghetti and cook al dente according to the package instructions. During the last minute, add the broccoli. Reserve 2 cups of pasta water and drain.

3. In a large skillet warm the oil over medium-low heat. Once hot, add the shallot and pistachios and sauté for 4 to 5 minutes until the shallot is tender and the pistachios are lightly toasted. Add about half of the feta and cook for another 1 to 2 minutes.

4. Transfer the pasta and broccoli to the pan along with 1 cup of the reserved pasta water. Continue to cook, tossing the pasta with the sauce until well combined. Gradually add more pasta water and continue tossing until the pasta is glossy and the sauce is your desired consistency.

5. Just before serving, add the remaining feta and toss once more to combine. Salt to taste, then serve with extra chopped pistachios sprinkled over the top.

YIELD: 6 SERVINGS | PREP: 15 MIN | REST: 30 MIN | COOK: 15 MIN

TAJÍN RANCH CHICKEN THIGHS

The best thing about these chicken thighs is their versatility—serve them with rice, tortillas, or greens like the Charred Corn Salad with Cilantro Dressing (pg. 121) or Crunchy Cabbage Slaw (pg. 243). The secret ingredient, milk powder, tenderizes the chicken and gives it that signature ranch flavor.

INGREDIENTS

1 tablespoon dry milk powder
1 tablespoon onion powder
1½ teaspoons garlic powder
1 tablespoon dried parsley
1½ teaspoons dried dill
1 teaspoon dried Mexican oregano
1 tablespoon Tajín, plus more for serving
2 tablespoons kosher salt
3 pounds chicken thighs, boneless and skinless
2 jalapeños
2 bell peppers, any color
2 bunches green onions
2 tablespoons extra-virgin olive oil

GUACAMOLE & ASSEMBLY

3 avocados
1 lime, juiced
Pinch of kosher salt
Pinch of ground cumin
Corn tortillas or rice, for serving

TIP: Gloves are a good idea when seasoning the chicken—Tajín has a way of sticking around on your hands.

DIRECTIONS

1. Make the seasoning by combining the milk powder, onion powder, garlic powder, parsley, dill, oregano, Tajín, and salt.

2. Pat the chicken thighs dry and sprinkle generously on both sides with the seasoning (you should use it all). Let the chicken rest at room temperature for 20 to 30 minutes.

3. Meanwhile, quarter and deseed the jalapeños and bell peppers and chop the green onions into 2-inch pieces.

4. Turn the oven on broil and situate a rack in the top quarter of the oven—the chicken should be only 3 to 4 inches from the broiler. Gently pat the chicken dry once more, just to remove any large spots of moisture, and drizzle both sides with the olive oil. Transfer the chicken to an 18 x 13-inch sheet pan and add the peppers, then place under the broiler.

5. Broil for 10 to 15 minutes, flipping the chicken halfway through, until the internal temperature reaches 165 degrees. Add the green onions to the sheet pan during the last 3 to 4 minutes of cooking.

6. Let the chicken rest while making the guacamole. Mash the avocados with the lime juice, salt, and cumin. Finely chop about one third of the charred jalapeños and green onions from the sheet pan and add them to the mashed avocado. Taste and adjust for salt.

7. To serve, sprinkle the chicken with more Tajín and plate either sliced or whole. Enjoy with the guacamole and corn tortillas or rice.

YIELD: 6 SERVINGS PREP: 20 MIN COOK: 45 MIN

SHEET PAN LASAGNA BOLOGNESE

On a chaotic weeknight, this lasagna comes together fast with a shortcut bolognese full of veggies. Poured right onto the sheet pan, the pasta looks a little unkempt—that is, until it comes out of the oven bubbling and golden, topped with ricotta and a few fresh basil leaves.

INGREDIENTS

3 tablespoons extra-virgin olive oil, divided
3 stalks celery
2 medium carrots
1 yellow onion
2 ½ cups fresh spinach, loosely packed
½ pound ground beef, 20% fat
½ pound sweet Italian sausage
2 ½ teaspoons kosher salt, divided
1 cup dry red wine
1 (28-ounce) can San Marzano tomatoes
1 pound dried lasagna noodles
4 cups grated mozzarella
1 cup whole-milk ricotta
Fresh basil, for serving

DIRECTIONS

1. Preheat the oven to 375 degrees and grease an 18 x 13-inch sheet pan with 1 tablespoon of the oil. Bring a large pot of heavily salted water to a boil.

2. Meanwhile, roughly chop the celery, carrots, and onion into large pieces and add them to a food processor. Process for about 1 minute until the veggies are very finely minced, then add the spinach and pulse for another 1 to 2 minutes until the mixture looks almost like a paste. Set aside.

3. To a large Dutch oven over medium-high heat, add the remaining 2 tablespoons oil. Once hot, add the ground beef, Italian sausage, and 1 teaspoon of the salt. Crumble the meat until fine and sauté until nearly cooked through, 4 to 5 minutes.

4. Add the veggie mixture to the meat along with the remaining 1 ½ teaspoons salt. Cook for another 6 to 8 minutes, stirring occasionally, until the moisture has evaporated.

5. Pour in the wine and tomatoes, hand-crushing the tomatoes as you add them to the pot. Stir to combine, then reduce the heat to low and cover. Let the sauce simmer while boiling the pasta.

6. Boil the lasagna sheets for about 4 minutes, or according to package instructions, until just softened and not yet al dente. Drain the pasta and add it to the sauce. Toss until each lasagna noodle is coated in sauce.

7. Add a little over half of the mozzarella to the pasta. Stir again to melt the cheese and incorporate it into the sauce. Pour the mixture onto the prepared sheet pan, then top with the remaining mozzarella.

8. Transfer to the oven and bake until bubbling and the edges of the exposed pasta are golden, 20 to 25 minutes. To serve, top with generous dollops of ricotta and whole basil leaves.

YIELD: 4 SERVINGS PREP: 40 MIN COOK: 10 MIN

SWISS "CHARRED" PORTOBELLO BOWLS

This bowl makes good use of your grill with a charred shallot that gets blitzed into the most incredible vinaigrette you've ever tasted. Pour it all over a bowl of brown rice stacked with smoky grilled almonds, Swiss chard, and meaty portobellos.

INGREDIENTS

GRILLED SHALLOT VINAIGRETTE

¾ cup extra-virgin olive oil, plus more for grilling
⅓ cup apple cider vinegar
1 tablespoon honey
1½ teaspoons dried thyme
1½ teaspoons kosher salt, divided
½ teaspoon granulated garlic
1 grilled shallot (see below)

PORTOBELLO BOWL ASSEMBLY

4 portobello mushroom caps, stems and gills removed
¾ cup Marcona almonds
1 head romaine
1 bunch Swiss chard
1 shallot
2 avocados
½ cup dried cherries
2 cups cooked brown rice

DIRECTIONS

1. Preheat the grill to 450 degrees over medium heat.

2. Make the vinaigrette by blending the oil, vinegar, honey, thyme, and ½ teaspoon of the salt. In a small bowl add the granulated garlic and the remaining 1 teaspoon salt. Remove ¼ cup of the vinaigrette and add it to the garlic and salt to make a marinade. Stir to combine.

3. Coat the mushroom caps with the marinade on both sides. Place the almonds on double-layered aluminum foil with raised edges.

4. Slice the romaine in half lengthwise and trim the stems from the Swiss chard. Slice the shallot in half through the root and remove the skin. Drizzle the romaine, chard, and shallots with olive oil and transfer to the grill, placing the shallot cut-side down. Place the almonds on the warming shelf or a cool burner.

5. With the lid open, grill the romaine and chard for about 60 seconds. Remove from the grill, close the lid, and leave the shallots and almonds to continue grilling for 2 minutes.

6. Place the portobello mushrooms on the grill. Close the lid and grill for 3 to 4 minutes, then flip the mushrooms and grill for another 3 minutes. Remove the mushrooms, shallots, and almonds from the grill.

7. Roughly chop the shallots and blend with the reserved vinaigrette. Chop the chard, romaine, and almonds, then dice the avocados and add everything to a large bowl. Add the dried cherries and toss to combine. Finally, slice the grilled portobellos.

8. To assemble the bowls, top the rice with salad, sliced portobello, and shallot vinaigrette.

150

YIELD: 4 SERVINGS PREP: 20 MIN COOK: 30 MIN

PLUM & FENNEL PORK CHOPS

Something special happens to plums when cooked with shaved fennel. Tossed together in a miso pan sauce and spooned over seared, bone-in pork chops, they develop a savory sweetness that is undeniably delicious.

INGREDIENTS

- 4 center-cut pork chops, bone-in (about 2 ½ pounds)
- 4 ½ teaspoons kosher salt, divided
- 1 fennel bulb, plus fronds for serving
- 4 plums, any variety
- 4 tablespoons unsalted butter, divided
- 1 tablespoon whole-grain mustard
- 1 tablespoon white miso paste
- ¾ cup low-sodium chicken stock

DIRECTIONS

1. Sprinkle the pork chops evenly on both sides with 4 teaspoons of the salt. Set aside to rest for 15 minutes.

2. While the pork rests, thinly slice the fennel bulb and slice the plums into eighths. Preheat a 12-inch cast-iron skillet over medium heat, then add 2 tablespoons of the butter. Once melted, transfer the fennel and plums to the pan and add the remaining ½ teaspoon salt.

3. Sauté the fennel and plums for about 10 minutes, or until the fennel is soft and starting to brown. Remove the fennel and plums from the pan, leaving behind any remaining butter. Increase the heat to medium-high.

4. Pat the pork chops very dry and transfer them to the skillet, working in batches if needed. Let the pork chops sear, undisturbed, for 4 to 5 minutes. Flip the pork chops and cook for an additional 4 to 5 minutes, or until the internal temperature reaches 145 degrees.

5. Remove the pork chops from the pan, reduce the heat to medium-low, and add the remaining 2 tablespoons butter. Transfer the plum and fennel back to the pan, along with the mustard, miso paste, and stock. Stir to combine, scraping up any brown bits at the bottom of the pan. Simmer for about 5 minutes, or until the sauce has reduced slightly. Remove from heat.

6. Return the pork chops to the pan, spooning the sauce over top. Garnish with fennel fronds and serve.

YIELD: 4 SERVINGS PREP: 30 MIN COOK: 25 MIN

GREEK HALLOUMI & CHICKEN SALAD

With just a quick sear on both sides, halloumi is as much a treat as it is a source of protein. Whenever I make this salad—which is often—I brown a few extra pieces of halloumi for the girls to snack on while I finish cooking. We love the marinated chicken, but you can easily leave it out to make the dish vegetarian.

INGREDIENTS

MEDITERRANEAN VINAIGRETTE & MARINADE

½ cup extra-virgin olive oil
¼ cup sherry vinegar
½ cup fresh oregano leaves, loosely packed
½ cup fresh mint leaves, loosely packed
1 garlic clove
4 teaspoons kosher salt

CHICKEN & HALLOUMI SALAD

1¾ pounds chicken breast, boneless and skinless
2 bell peppers, any color
1 pound on-the-vine tomatoes
1 English cucumber
½ red onion
2 teaspoons kosher salt
8 ounces halloumi
1 tablespoon extra-virgin olive oil

DIRECTIONS

1. In a small bowl whisk together the oil and vinegar. Finely mince the oregano, mint, and garlic, then whisk into the vinaigrette. Transfer ⅓ cup of the vinaigrette to a bowl or plastic bag, then add the salt to create a marinade. Set aside the remaining vinaigrette for later.

2. Butterfly the chicken breasts, then add them to the marinade and let sit at room temperature for 30 minutes.

3. While the chicken marinates, dice the peppers, tomatoes, cucumber, and onion. Use a colander to rinse the diced onion under cold water. Transfer all of the diced vegetables to the colander with the onion and place over a large bowl. Toss the veggies with the salt and set aside to drain off any excess liquid.

4. Dice the halloumi into ½-inch pieces and preheat a skillet over medium heat. Add the oil and the halloumi. Let the halloumi sear for about 3 minutes, then toss and sear for another 3 minutes. Once at least 2 sides of the halloumi are browned, remove them from the pan.

5. To the same pan, add the marinated chicken. Cover the pan and sear for 5 minutes, then flip the chicken and sear, uncovered, for another 5 minutes. Continue flipping the chicken every 5 minutes, covering while it cooks, until the internal temperature reaches 165 degrees. Remove the chicken from the pan and let it rest.

6. Transfer the drained vegetables and seared halloumi to a large bowl and toss with the remaining vinaigrette. Slice or chop the chicken, add it to the salad, and serve.

YIELD: 6 SERVINGS PREP: 20 MIN COOK: 45 MIN

ROASTED CHICKEN WITH LEMON ORZOTTO

It's hard to believe this dish takes only an hour to prepare. The chicken thighs are savory with golden skin, while orzotto takes the best of risotto and makes it weeknight friendly. With lemons cooked down until mellow and sweet, it's a comforting dinner that feels much fancier than it really is.

INGREDIENTS

- 2 teaspoons granulated sugar
- 7 teaspoons kosher salt, divided
- 3 ½ pounds chicken thighs, bone-in and skin-on
- 1 lemon, plus more for serving
- 1 yellow onion
- 2 tablespoons fresh sage leaves, loosely packed
- 3 tablespoons extra-virgin olive oil, divided
- 6 cups chicken stock
- 1 pound orzo
- 1 cup grated sharp white cheddar
- ½ cup whole milk

DIRECTIONS

1. Preheat the oven to 425 degrees. In a small bowl combine the sugar with 5 teaspoons of the salt. Sprinkle over both sides of the chicken thighs and let rest while preparing the remaining ingredients.

2. Trim the pithy ends off the lemon and cut in half lengthwise. Slice the lemon as thinly as possible into half-moons, then thinly slice the onion and finely chop the sage. Set aside the lemon, onion, and sage in a bowl.

3. Pat the chicken dry and brush the skin with 1 tablespoon of the oil. Place the chicken on an 18 x 13-inch sheet pan and roast for 40 to 45 minutes, until the skin is golden and crisp and the internal temperature registers 165 degrees.

4. Meanwhile, make the orzotto. In a small saucepan add the chicken stock and bring to a simmer over medium heat. Cover and reduce heat to low.

5. Meanwhile, in a large skillet over medium heat, add the remaining 2 tablespoons oil as well as the sliced lemon, onions, and sage. Once sizzling, cook for 8 to 10 minutes, stirring frequently until soft. Add the orzo and toast for 3 minutes.

6. Add the warmed stock and the remaining 2 teaspoons salt to the skillet. Reduce the heat to low to maintain a steady simmer. Cook for 12 to 14 minutes, stirring frequently, until the orzo is tender and the liquid is mostly absorbed.

7. Remove the pan from the heat and add the cheese, a handful at a time, stirring until melted. Finally, add the milk and stir to combine. Serve the orzotto topped with a roasted chicken thigh. If desired, garnish with lemon zest.

ACKNOWLEDGMENTS

Bringing this book from scribbled notes to candlelit tables has been a true collaboration. Katie Calton poured her time, talent, and love of food into every recipe development and late-night brainstorm, turning each day in my messy kitchen into pure joy. Lucy Call translated flavor into imagery with her discerning eye, while Kristine Monson fussed over every vignette—down to the place cards and the fold of every linen. Danielle Munz added calm, meticulous support to the styling process and Ashley Beyer made sure each flower was arranged with care. Kortney Eggertz shaped my ideas and vision into cookbook form, one that can be passed down for generations. The warm glow belongs to Trenton Davis and Spencer Goff, whose mastery of light set the tone for every shot. Thank you to Fatima Khawaja for cross-testing with precision and care. My agent, Bill Stankey, championed this project from proposal to print, and Matt Baugher—along with the entire Harper Horizon team—believed in its promise from the very first pitch. Chloe Stauffer kept our many moving parts on track, and Julia Tran and Lina Barrios polished every photograph with a keen eye.

My late grandmother, Gloria Miller, first showed me that love can be shared in the form of chocolate pie, and her legacy lives in these pages. My dad followed suit with steady encouragement, honest feedback, and fearless forks at the ready. To my mom, who insists every occasion deserves a touch of something special and taught me how to elevate everyday meals with warmth and care—thank you for laying the foundation for it all. Syd, thank you for tasting every bite (even when you had already tried five previous iterations) and cheering me on without pause; your unwavering support seasons everything I do. Wren, Ivy, and Margot, thank you for always sneaking the cookie dough to boost my confidence and being my favorite sous chefs.

To the entire team—thank you for lending your skills, work ethic, and heart; may these pages return your generosity in every shared bite.

RECIPE INDEX

A All-Purpose Dough, 187

ALMONDS
Loaded Everyday Granola, 41
Strawberry Tabbouleh, 59
Farro Arugula Salad, 71
Grilled Squash with Whipped Feta, 119
Swiss "Charred" Portobello Bowls, 319

APPETIZERS/SNACKS
Apple & Brie Bites, 103
Baguette with Balsamic Dipping Oil, 105
Blackberry Gouda Skewers, 167
Grilled Garlic Bread, 133
Picnic Potato Chips, 169
Whipped Ricotta Crostini, 43
White Bean Hummus with Walnut Oil, 39

APPLE
Apple & Brie Bites, 103
Guide to Charcuterie, 199
Mixed Berry Slab Pie, 209
Pomegranate Sangria, 305

Apple & Brie Bites, 103

Arnold Palmer, 137

ARUGULA
Farro Arugula Salad, 71
Peach Burrata Salad, 155
Savory Dutch Baby, 255
Turkey Beach Sandwich with Kale Cashew Pesto, 165
Autumn Sweet Potato Salad, 185

ASPARAGUS
Melt-in-Your-Mouth Salmon with Asparagus, 79

AVOCADO
Butter Lettuce Salad, 83
Chicken Tortilla Soup, 221
Market BLTA, 57
Swiss "Charred" Portobello Bowls, 319
Tajín Ranch Chicken Thighs, 315

B **BACON**
Autumn Sweet Potato Salad, 185
Market BLTA, 57

Baguette with Balsamic Dipping Oil, 105

BALSAMIC VINEGAR
Baguette with Balsamic Dipping Oil, 105
Blackberry Gouda Skewers, 167
Honey Balsamic Vinaigrette, 155
Turkey Beach Sandwich with Kale Cashew Pesto, 165

BASIL
Apple & Brie Bites, 103
Baguette with Balsamic Dipping Oil, 105
Basil & Lemon-Pepper Mayo, 57
Basil Garlic Knots, 85
Go-To Tomato Sauce, 145
Kale Cashew Pesto, 165
Roasted Red Pepper & Tortellini Soup, 223
Sheet Pan Lasagna Bolognese, 317
Vegetable Frittata, 37

Basil & Lemon-Pepper Mayo, 57

Basil Garlic Knots, 85

BEANS
Beef Pot Pie Soup, 227
Brown Butter Green Beans with Crunchy Breadcrumbs, 191
Butternut Squash Enchiladas, 239
Caesar Salad with Crispy Chickpeas, 301
Chicken Tortilla Soup, 221
White Bean Hummus with Walnut Oil, 39

BEEF
Beef Pot Pie Soup, 227
Cranberry Braised Short Ribs, 285
Sheet Pan Lasagna Bolognese, 317
Syd's Sliders for a Crowd, 115
Tender Grilled Flank Steak, 69

Beef Pot Pie Soup, 227

BEETS
Citrus & Fennel Salad, 259

BERRIES
Blackberry Gouda Skewers, 167
Strawberry Tabbouleh, 59
Mixed Berry Slab Pie, 209
Lemon Berry Pavlova, 107
Strawberries & Cream Cake, 135

Blackberry Gouda Skewers, 167

BREADS
All-Purpose Dough, 187
Basil Garlic Knots, 85
Golden Crescent Rolls, 187
Grilled Garlic Bread, 133

Gruyère Brioche Stuffing, 193
Mini Cinnamon Rolls, 257
Perfect Pizza Dough, 143
Whole Wheat Focaccia, 53

BREAKFAST
Loaded Everyday Granola, 41
Mini Cinnamon Rolls, 257
Rosy Mimosas, 47
Savory Dutch Baby, 255
Vegetable Frittata, 37

BROCCOLI/BROCCOLINI
Broccoli Pistachio Spaghetti, 313
Garlicky Cod & Quinoa, 311
Vegetable Frittata, 37

Broccoli Pistachio Spaghetti, 313

BROTH
Chicken Tortilla Soup, 221

BROWN BUTTER
Brown Butter Citrus Cake, 291
Brown Butter Frosting, 291
Brown Butter Green Beans with Crunchy Breadcrumbs, 191
Brown Butter Pecan Pie, 213

Brown Butter Citrus Cake, 291

Brown Butter Frosting, 291

Brown Butter Green Beans with Crunchy Breadcrumbs, 191

Brown Butter Pecan Pie, 213

BRUSSELS SPROUTS
Autumn Sweet Potato Salad, 185

BURRATA
Peach Burrata Salad, 155

Butter Lettuce Salad, 83

BUTTERMILK
Buttermilk Chive Dressing, 83
Strawberries & Cream Cake, 135
Cornbread Bundts with Rosemary Honey Butter, 233

Buttermilk Chive Dressing, 83

Butternut Squash Enchiladas, 239

C

CABBAGE
Crunchy Cabbage Slaw, 243

Cacio e Pepe Mashed Potatoes, 287

Caesar Salad with Crispy Chickpeas, 301

Caesar Dressing, 301

CAKE
Brown Butter Citrus Cake, 291
Four-Layer Southern Coconut Cake, 87
Grandma Glo's Cola Cake, 123
No-Bake Bay Leaf Cheesecake, 45
Strawberries & Cream Cake, 135

CARROTS
Beef Pot Pie Soup, 227
Cranberry Braised Short Ribs, 285
Crunchy Cabbage Slaw, 243
Sheet Pan Lasagna Bolognese, 317

Cast-Iron Piccata, 99

Cauliflower Corn Chowder, 225

Charred Corn Salad with Cilantro Dressing, 121

CHEESE (*See also* Goat Cheese, Mozzarella, Parmigiano-Reggiano)
Fontina Apple Pizza, 147
Broccoli Pistachio Spaghetti, 313
Butternut Squash Enchiladas, 239
Cacio e Pepe Mashed Potatoes, 287
Caesar Salad with Crispy Chickpeas, 301
Farro Arugula Salad, 71
Garden Couscous Salad, 101
Green Goddess Pizza, 151
Grilled Garlic Bread, 133
Grilled Squash with Whipped Feta, 119
Gruyère Brioche Stuffing, 193
Hot Honey Pizza, 149
No-Bake Bay Leaf Cheesecake, 45
Peach Burrata Salad, 155
Roasted Chicken with Lemon Orzotto, 325
Sausage & Mushroom Pizza, 153
Savory Dutch Baby, 255
Sheet Pan Lasagna Bolognese, 317
Silky Mascarpone Pappardelle, 299
Strawberry Tabbouleh, 59
Vegetable Frittata, 37
Whipped Ricotta Crostini, 43

Cherry Chocolate Mousse, 303

CHICKEN
Butternut Squash Enchiladas, 239
Cast-Iron Piccata, 99
Chicken Tortilla Soup, 221
Greek Halloumi & Chicken Salad, 323
Roasted Chicken with Lemon Orzotto, 325
Tajín Ranch Chicken Thighs, 315

Chicken Tortilla Soup, 221

Chipotle Burger Sauce, 115

CHOCOLATE
Cherry Chocolate Mousse, 303
Chocolate Hazelnut Meringue Pie, 203
Chocolate Peppermint Sandwich Cookies, 265
Grandma Glo's Cola Cake, 123
Loaded Everyday Granola, 41
Magic Crispy Bars, 245
McGee's Ultimate Brownie, 171
S'mores Cookie Skillet, 157
Shea's Favorite Chocolate Chip Cookie, 63
Triple-Chocolate Hot Chocolate, 279
White Chocolate Chewy Gingersnaps, 271

Chocolate Hazelnut Meringue Pie, 203

Chocolate Peppermint Sandwich Cookies, 265

Cilantro Dressing, 121

Citrus & Fennel Salad, 259

CINNAMON
Mini Cinnamon Rolls, 257
Pumpkin-Pie Cheesecake Bars, 207
White Chocolate Chewy Gingersnaps, 271
Classic Seafood Boil, 131

COCKTAILS/MOCKTAILS
Arnold Palmer, 137
Pomegranate Sangria, 305
Rosy Mimosas, 47
Watermelon Ranch Water, 125

COCONUT
Coconut Cream Cheese Frosting, 87
Four-Layer Southern Coconut Cake, 87
Loaded Everyday Granola, 41
Magic Crispy Bars, 245

Coconut Cream Cheese Frosting, 87

Confetti Birthday Blondies, 73

COOKIES/BARS
Chocolate Peppermint Sandwich Cookies, 265
Confetti Birthday Blondies, 73
Cookie Butter Blossoms, 275
Cream Cheese Spritz Wreaths, 277
Magic Crispy Bars, 245
McGee's Ultimate Brownie, 171
Pumpkin-Pie Cheesecake Bars, 207
S'mores Cookie Skillet, 157
Shea's Favorite Chocolate Chip Cookie, 63
Snowball Sandies, 269
White Chocolate Chewy Gingersnaps, 271

Cookie Butter Blossoms, 275

CORN
Cauliflower Corn Chowder, 225
Charred Corn Salad with Cilantro Dressing, 121
Classic Seafood Boil, 131

Cornbread Bundts with Rosemary Honey Butter, 233

CRANBERRY
Cream Cheese Spritz Wreaths, 277
Cranberry Braised Short Ribs, 285
Pomegranate Sangria (as a mocktail), 305

Cranberry Braised Short Ribs, 285

CREAM CHEESE
Coconut Cream Cheese Frosting, 87
Cream Cheese Spritz Wreaths, 277
Maple Cream Cheese Frosting, 257
No-Bake Bay Leaf Cheesecake, 45
Pumpkin-Pie Cheesecake Bars, 207

Cream Cheese Spritz Wreaths, 277

Crunchy Cabbage Slaw, 243

CUCUMBER
Crunchy Cabbage Slaw, 243
Garden Couscous Salad, 101
Greek Halloumi & Chicken Salad, 323

Quick Pickles, 115
Tzatziki Cucumbers, 61

Cumin Lime Vinaigrette, 243

D

DESSERTS (*See also* Cakes, Cookies/Bars, Pies)
Cherry Chocolate Mousse, 303
Lemon Berry Pavlova, 107
Salted Vanilla Bean Ice Cream, 159
Triple-Chocolate Hot Chocolate, 279

DRESSINGS
Basil & Lemon-Pepper Mayo, 57
Buttermilk Chive Dressing, 83
Caesar Dressing, 301
Chipotle Burger Sauce, 115
Cilantro Dressing, 121
Cumin Lime Vinaigrette, 243
Fig Vinaigrette, 71
Ginger Tahini Dressing, 289
Green Goddess Dressing, 151
Grilled Shallot Vinaigrette, 319
Honey Balsamic Vinaigrette, 155
Maple Citrus Vinaigrette, 185
Mediterranean Vinaigrette & Marinade, 323
Kale Cashew Pesto, 165
Toasted Walnut Oil, 39

E

EGGS
Savory Dutch Baby, 255
Vegetable Frittata, 37

Essential Roasted Turkey, 181

F

Farro Arugula Salad, 71

FENNEL
Citrus & Fennel Salad, 259
Plum & Fennel Pork Chops, 321

FETA
Broccoli Pistachio Spaghetti, 313
Grilled Squash with Whipped Feta, 119
Strawberry Tabbouleh, 59

Fig Vinaigrette, 71

FISH (*See also* Seafood)
Garlicky Cod & Quinoa, 311
Melt-in-Your-Mouth Salmon with Asparagus, 79

Fontina Apple Pizza, 147

Four-Layer Southern Coconut Cake, 87

G

Garden Couscous Salad, 101

GARLIC
Basil Garlic Knots, 85
Garlicky Cod & Quinoa, 311
Grilled Garlic Bread, 133
Signature Herb Butter, 131

Garlicky Cod & Quinoa, 311

GINGER
Ginger Tahini Dressing, 289
Melt-in-Your-Mouth Salmon with Asparagus, 79
Turkey & Wild Rice Soup, 231
White Chocolate Chewy Gingersnaps, 271

Go-To Tomato Sauce, 145

GOAT CHEESE
Green Goddess Pizza, 151
Guide to Charcuterie, 199
Vegetable Frittata, 37

Golden Crescent Rolls, 187

GRAHAM CRACKERS
Chocolate Hazelnut Meringue Pie, 203
No-Bake Bay Leaf Cheesecake, 45
S'mores Cookie Skillet, 157

GRAINS
Farro Arugula Salad, 71
Garlicky Cod & Quinoa, 311
Loaded Everyday Granola, 41
Strawberry Tabbouleh, 59
Swiss "Charred" Portobello Bowls, 319
Turkey & Wild Rice Soup, 231

Grandma Glo's Cola Cake, 123

GRAPEFRUIT
Brown Butter Citrus Cake, 291

Greek Halloumi & Chicken Salad, 323

GREEN BEANS
Beef Pot Pie Soup, 227
Brown Butter Green Beans with Crunchy Breadcrumbs, 191

Green Goddess Dressing, 151

Green Goddess Pizza, 151

Grilled Garlic Bread, 133

Grilled Shallot Vinaigrette, 319

Grilled Squash with Whipped Feta, 119

Gruyère Brioche Stuffing, 193

Guide to Charcuterie, 199

H

HAZELNUTS
Chocolate Hazelnut Meringue Pie, 203
Citrus & Fennel Salad, 259
Loaded Everyday Granola, 41

HERBS (fresh, *see also* Basil)
Baguette with Balsamic Dipping Oil, 105
Garden Couscous Salad, 101
Green Goddess Pizza, 151
Grilled Squash with Whipped Feta, 119
Lemony Smashed Potatoes, 81
Melt-in-Your-Mouth Salmon with Asparagus, 79
Signature Herb Butter, 131
Strawberry Tabbouleh, 59
Tzatziki Cucumbers, 61
White Bean Hummus with Walnut Oil, 39

Herbes de Provence Croutons, 227

Honey Balsamic Vinaigrette, 155

Hot Honey Pizza, 149

J

JALAPEÑOS
Butternut Squash Enchiladas, 239
Cilantro Dressing, 121
Tajín Ranch Chicken Thighs, 315
Watermelon Ranch Water, 125

K

KALE
Turkey & Wild Rice Soup, 231
Turkey Beach Sandwich with Kale Cashew Pesto, 165
Vegetable Frittata, 37
Winter Salad with Tahini Dressing, 289

Kale Cashew Pesto, 165

L

LEEKS
Cauliflower Corn Chowder, 225
Cranberry Braised Short Ribs, 285

LEMON
Arnold Palmer, 137
Basil & Lemon-Pepper Mayo, 57
Grilled Squash with Whipped Feta, 119
Lemon Berry Pavlova, 107
Lemony Smashed Potatoes, 81
Olive Oil Lemon Curd, 107
Roasted Chicken with Lemon Orzotto, 325

Lemon Berry Pavlova, 107

Lemony Smashed Potatoes, 81

LIME
Crunchy Cabbage Slaw, 243
Tender Grilled Flank Steak, 69
Watermelon Ranch Water, 125

Loaded Everyday Granola, 41

LUNCH
Crunchy Cabbage Slaw, 243
Garden Couscous Salad, 101
Farro Arugula Salad, 71
Market BLTA, 57
Strawberry Tabbouleh, 59
Turkey Beach Sandwich with Kale Cashew Pesto, 165

M

Magic Crispy Bars, 245

Maple Citrus Vinaigrette, 185

Maple Cream Cheese Frosting, 257

Market BLTA, 57

McGee's Ultimate Brownie, 171

MEAT (*See also* Beef, Chicken, Pork, and Turkey)

Mediterranean Vinaigrette & Marinade, 323

MELON
Blackberry Gouda Skewers, 167
Watermelon Ranch Water, 125

Melt-in-Your-Mouth Salmon with Asparagus, 79

Mini Cinnamon Rolls, 257

Mixed Berry Slab Pie, 209

MOZZARELLA
Hot Honey Pizza, 149
Sausage & Mushroom Pizza, 153
Sheet Pan Lasagna Bolognese, 317

MUSHROOMS
Sausage & Mushroom Pizza, 153
Silky Mascarpone Pappardelle, 299
Swiss "Charred" Portobello Bowls, 319
Turkey & Wild Rice Soup, 231
Must-Have Gravy, 181

N

NUTS (*See also* Almonds, Hazelnuts, Pistachios, Walnuts)
Autumn Sweet Potato Salad, 185
Blackberry Gouda Skewers, 167
Broccoli Pistachio Spaghetti, 313
Brown Butter Pecan Pie, 213
Chocolate Hazelnut Meringue Pie, 203
Citrus & Fennel Salad, 259
Crunchy Cabbage Slaw, 243
Farro Arugula Salad, 71
Garden Couscous Salad, 101
Grilled Squash with Whipped Feta, 119
Guide to Charcuterie, 199
Kale Cashew Pesto, 165
Loaded Everyday Granola, 41
Peach Burrata Salad, 155
Snowball Sandies, 269
Strawberry Tabbouleh, 59
Swiss "Charred" Portobello Bowls, 319
Toasted Walnut Oil, 39
White Bean Hummus with Walnut Oil, 39

No-Bake Bay Leaf Cheesecake, 45

O

OLIVE OIL
Baguette with Balsamic Dipping Oil, 105
Olive Oil Lemon Curd, 107
Toasted Walnut Oil, 39
Tzatziki Cucumbers, 61
Whole Wheat Focaccia, 53
Olive Oil Lemon Curd, 107

ORANGE
Brown Butter Citrus Cake, 291
Cast-Iron Piccata, 99
Citrus & Fennel Salad, 259
Essential Roasted Turkey, 181
Maple Citrus Vinaigrette, 185
Pomegranate Sangria, 305
Rosy Mimosas, 47
White Chocolate Chewy Gingersnaps, 271

P

PARMIGIANO-REGGIANO
Caesar Salad with Crispy Chickpeas, 301
Grilled Garlic Bread, 133
Lemony Smashed Potatoes, 81
Roasted Red Pepper & Tortellini Soup, 223
Savory Dutch Baby, 255

PASTA
Broccoli Pistachio Spaghetti, 313
Garden Couscous Salad, 101
Roasted Red Pepper & Tortellini Soup, 223
Silky Mascarpone Pappardelle, 299
Sheet Pan Lasagna Bolognese, 317

PASTRY
Herbes de Provence Croutons, 227
Reliably Flaky Pie Crust, 201

Peach Burrata Salad, 155

PEARS
Guide to Charcuterie, 199
Winter Salad with Tahini Dressing, 289

PECORINO
Cacio e Pepe Mashed Potatoes, 287

PEPPER(S)
Chicken Tortilla Soup, 221
Greek Halloumi & Chicken Salad, 323
Roasted Red Pepper & Tortellini Soup, 223
Tajín Ranch Chicken Thighs, 315

Peppermint Frosting, 265

Perfect Pizza Dough, 143

PISTACHIOS
Broccoli Pistachio Spaghetti, 313
Garden Couscous Salad, 101

Picnic Potato Chips, 169

PIES
Brown Butter Pecan Pie, 213
Chocolate Hazelnut Meringue Pie, 203
Mixed Berry Slab Pie, 209
Pumpkin-Pie Cheesecake Bars, 207
Reliably Flaky Pie Crust, 201

PIZZA
Fontina Apple Pizza, 147
Green Goddess Pizza, 151
Hot Honey Pizza, 149
Perfect Pizza Dough, 143

Sausage & Mushroom Pizza, 153

Plum & Fennel Pork Chops, 321

POMEGRANATE
Citrus & Fennel Salad, 259
Guide to Charcuterie, 199
Pomegranate Sangria, 305

Pomegranata Sangria, 305

PORK
Apple & Brie Bites, 103
Autumn Sweet Potato Salad, 185
Classic Seafood Boil, 131
Cauliflower Corn Chowder, 225
Guide to Charcuterie, 199
Hot Honey Pizza, 149
Market BLTA, 57
Plum & Fennel Pork Chops, 321
Roasted Red Pepper & Tortellini Soup, 223
Sausage & Mushroom Pizza, 153
Savory Dutch Baby, 255
Sheet Pan Lasagna Bolognese, 317

POTATOES
Autumn Sweet Potato Salad, 185
Beef Pot Pie Soup, 227
Cacio e Pepe Mashed Potatoes, 287
Classic Seafood Boil, 131
Essential Roasted Turkey, 181
Lemony Smashed Potatoes, 81
Picnic Potato Chips, 169

Pumpkin-Pie Cheesecake Bars, 207

Q

Quick Pickles, 115

R

RADICCHIO
Winter Salad with Tahini Dressing, 289
Reliably Flaky Pie Crust, 201

RICOTTA
Hot Honey Pizza, 149
No-Bake Bay Leaf Cheesecake, 45
Savory Dutch Baby, 255
Sheet Pan Lasagna Bolognese, 317
Whipped Ricotta Crostini, 43

Roasted Chicken with Lemon Orzotto, 325

ROASTED RED PEPPERS
Roasted Red Pepper & Tortellini Soup, 223
Turkey Beach Sandwich with Kale Cashew Pesto, 165

S

Roasted Red Pepper & Tortellini Soup, 223

Rosemary Honey Butter, 233

Rosy Mimosas, 47

S

SALADS/GREENS
Autumn Sweet Potato Salad, 185
Blackberry Gouda Skewers, 167
Butter Lettuce Salad, 83
Caesar Salad with Crispy Chickpeas, 301
Charred Corn Salad with Cilantro Dressing, 121
Citrus & Fennel Salad, 259
Crunchy Cabbage Slaw, 243
Farro Arugula Salad, 71
Garden Couscous Salad, 101
Greek Halloumi & Chicken Salad, 323
Peach Burrata Salad, 155
Strawberry Tabbouleh, 59
Swiss "Charred" Portobello Bowls, 319
Winter Salad with Tahini Dressing, 289

Salted Vanilla Bean Ice Cream, 159

SANDWICHES
Market BLTA, 57
Syd's Sliders for a Crowd, 115
Turkey Beach Sandwich with Kale Cashew Pesto, 165

Sausage & Mushroom Pizza, 153

Savory Dutch Baby, 255

SEAFOOD
Classic Seafood Boil, 131

SEEDS
Butter Lettuce Salad, 83
Charred Corn Salad with Cilantro Dressing, 121
Loaded Everyday Granola, 41
Tzatziki Cucumbers, 61
Winter Salad with Tahini Dressing, 289

Semolina Breadcrumbs, 289

Shea's Favorite Chocolate Chip Cookie, 63

Sheet Pan Lasagna Bolognese, 317

Signature Herb Butter, 131

Silky Mascarpone
Pappardelle, 299

S'mores Cookie Skillet, 157

Snowball Sandies, 269

SOUPS
Beef Pot Pie Soup, 227
Chicken Tortilla Soup, 221
Cauliflower Corn Chowder, 225
Turkey & Wild Rice Soup, 231

SPINACH
Roasted Red Pepper & Tortellini Soup, 223
Silky Mascarpone Pappardelle, 299
Sheet Pan Lasagna Bolognese, 317

SQUASH
Butternut Squash Enchiladas, 239
Grilled Squash with Whipped Feta, 119
Turkey & Wild Rice Soup, 231

Strawberries & Cream Cake, 135

Strawberry Tabbouleh, 59

Swiss "Charred" Portobello Bowls, 319

Syd's Sliders for a Crowd, 115

T

TAHINI
White Bean Hummus with Walnut Oil, 39
Winter Salad with Tahini Dressing, 289
Tajín Ranch Chicken Thighs, 315

Tender Grilled Flank Steak, 69

Toasted Walnut Oil, 39

TOMATO
Butternut Squash Enchiladas, 239
Charred Corn Salad with Cilantro Dressing, 121
Go-To Tomato Sauce, 145
Greek Halloumi & Chicken Salad, 323
Market BLTA, 57
Sheet Pan Lasagna Bolognese, 317

Triple-Chocolate Hot Chocolate, 279

TURKEY
Essential Roasted Turkey, 181
Turkey & Wild Rice Soup, 231
Turkey Beach Sandwich with Kale Cashew Pesto, 165

Tzatziki Cucumbers, 61

V

Vegetable Frittata, 37

W

WALNUTS
Blackberry Gouda Skewers, 167
Peach Burrata Salad, 155
Snowball Sandies, 269
White Bean Hummus with Walnut Oil, 39

WATERCRESS
Fontina Apple Pizza, 147

Watermelon Ranch Water, 125

Whipped Ricotta Crostini, 43
White Bean Hummus with Walnut Oil, 39
White Chocolate Chewy Gingersnaps, 271

Whole Wheat Focaccia, 53

Winter Salad with Tahini Dressing, 289

Y

YOGURT
Tzatziki Cucumbers, 61